Mindfulness Techniques

Practice Mindfulness Meditation and How to Live Life In The Moment

(Practical methods to Stress-Proof your mind from Depression)

Ryan Anderson

Published by Rob Miles

© **Ryan Anderson**

All Rights Reserved

Mindfulness Techniques: Practice Mindfulness Meditation and How to Live Life In The Moment (Practical methods to Stress-Proof your mind from Depression)

ISBN 978-1-990084-09-6

All rights reserved. No part of this guide may be reproduced in any form without permission in writing from the publisher except in the case of brief quotations embodied in critical articles or reviews.

Legal & Disclaimer

The information contained in this book is not designed to replace or take the place of any form of medicine or professional medical advice. The information in this book has been provided for educational and entertainment purposes only.

The information contained in this book has been compiled from sources deemed reliable, and it is accurate to the best of the Author's knowledge; however, the Author cannot guarantee its accuracy and validity and cannot be held liable for any errors or omissions. Changes are periodically made to this book. You must consult your doctor or get professional medical advice before using any of the suggested remedies, techniques, or information in this book.

Upon using the information contained in this book, you agree to hold harmless the Author from and against any damages, costs, and expenses, including any legal fees potentially resulting from the application of any of the information provided by this guide. This disclaimer applies to any damages or injury caused by the use and application, whether directly or indirectly, of any advice or information presented, whether for breach of contract, tort, negligence, personal injury, criminal intent, or under any other cause of action.

You agree to accept all risks of using the information presented inside this book. You need to consult a professional medical practitioner in order to ensure you are both able and healthy enough to participate in this program.

Table of Contents

INTRODUCTION 1

CHAPTER 1: AN INTRODUCTION 3

CHAPTER 2: RECOGNIZE THE MINDFUL TEACHERS IN YOUR LIFE 13

CHAPTER 3: SETTING GOALS 19

CHAPTER 4: PANIC ATTACKS 26

CHAPTER 5: EXAMPLES OF MINDFULNESS IN YOUR LIFE . 43

CHAPTER 6: THE HISTORY OF MINDFULNESS 52

CHAPTER 7: BENEFITS OF MINDFULNESS 67

CHAPTER 8: THE PHYSICAL BENEFITS OF MEDITATION 73

CHAPTER 9: BREAKING FREE 94

CHAPTER 10: HOW TO LISTEN TO YOUR BODY: SOMATIC MINDFULNESS AND KUNDALINI MEDITATION 101

CHAPTER 11: THE MIRACLE OF MINDFULNESS 120

CHAPTER 12: THE NEW YOU – DRESSING FOR SUCCESS AND MORE 123

CHAPTER 13: PRACTICING MEDITATION 129

CHAPTER 14: MINDFUL LISTENING 152

CHAPTER 15: SETTING GOALS 154

CHAPTER 16: WAYS TO FIND INSTANT CALM AND OVERCOME ANXIETY 162

CHAPTER 17: COMMON CHALLENGES YOU WILL ENCOUNTER 170

CONCLUSION 181

Introduction

If you are holding this book in your hands, then you are looking for answers.
This book does not contain answers.
It contains a path that will lead to answers.
The answers are within you.
Give yourself a chance - take the book home, read in a relaxed home environment.
It does not take a lot of time, but it will save enough of it for a real search.
Are you a professional, helping others? Read this book and tell your customers about it.
Perhaps it will save you time and help improve your interaction in the professional field.
Are you a manager? Employees practicing a more conscious lifestyle and as a result of practicing meditation, become less susceptible to stress, more stable in work,

and give out a better product in a shorter time.

The book unites the author and reader with the general concept of "we." This involves a joint search for solutions and interaction. The writer and the reader are interconnected. Without a writer, there is no book, but there is no book without a reader. Together we make the book a reality. When the concept of "you" is used, when instructions are given, then there is a division into the one who knows something and those who are taught.

This is not quite the right approach - because we learn together. Creating the text, the author collects the accumulated experience and reveals something new, and the one who reads the text adopts this experience - something new comes into his inner world. We are united in this process through writing and reading.

Chapter 1: An Introduction

Any discussion or attempt to understand meditation needs to start from consciousness along with space-time. The three concepts are inextricably tied together where each individual's consciousness is tied to a point in space and time.

Consciousness, on its own, is a commonly misunderstood concept. Consciousness is not a thing. It is abstract and only provides evidence from its own existence. It is self-evident. If you asked me to prove consciousness, I can't. But we both know that it is there. In the same way, consciousness is only a small part of the mind.

The mind, on the other hand, needs to be distinguished from the brain. The brain is the physical organ that we know resides in the cranial vault and extends a little lower to the base of the skull. However, the brain is not the mind. The brain is physical. The mind is abstract.

Consciousness is a part of the mind making it abstract. It is an abstract energy that causes physical realities in this world. Think about it this way, your abstract consciousness allows you to imagine. If you take that imagination and build what you've imagined—from nothingness, comes something. If I imagine building a great dam across the Amazon River, that imagination is not physical and thus it is abstract. Once I put tools to material and build the functioning dam, that abstract idea now becomes reality - from nothingness to something.

The typical human being is a conduit for the abstract to become reality.

Coming back to the consciousness, we understand that it is subject to interference from the physical world and the abstract. On one end of the conduit is the physical world - a world that you can touch, see, feel, smell, and hear. On the other end of the conduit is the cosmic world that cannot be touched and felt.

You can see this when you look at the concept of electromagnetic radiation. The frequencies that span the entire range cannot be seen by the human eye. We are not able to perceive it, but it's there. We can only perceive a small part of it and we call that visible light. The rest, are lost to our senses - but lost to us. In the same way, the world we perceive is only done so by our collective senses, but there is more to that. Our consciousness understands what we can physically perceive. What about the rest? What do we use to understand the other dimensions? Think of consciousness as the phenomenon that envelops our current space and time - the physical world in this one moment in time. But what about other moments in time and other physical aspects? What about the moment, in time and space, ahead of us, behind us and beside us? What do we use to perceive those? That is the perspective of the concept that we will call the subconscious.

To put it simply, the conscious looks at only one point in space and time - it looks at the here and now, and nothing else. The subconscious on the other hand looks at everything else. We will revisit this in the next chapter, as we go deeper into meditation and mindfulness.

Deep Dive

When we are first born, our consciousness is built from the physical world around us. We acquire character, thoughts, personalities and imaginations - all based on the image structure of our physical brain and the world we see outside. But there is also something more. We seem to call this something "more", imagination. Imagination is derived from two sources. The first source is the mind's ability to combine different ingredients to see what happens. When it happens, it's like putting a red dye into blue dye to see the color change. We know from grade school, you get purple, but the first time someone did that on their own, they didn't know what the result would be. We only imagined putting it together, and then we would draw a blank.

There is also the second kind of imagination. Einstein was talking about this imagination. This is the powerful cosmic imagination that takes grains of sand and builds great pyramids. This is also the imagination, which gives us things like the Theory of Relativity, Black Holes and everything that we cannot see, touch, feel or fathom. It is an imagination connected to the universe. The part that our consciousness cannot fathom.

In the Perspective of Meditation

To understand meditation we need to erect a construct of terms that will be consistent throughout the chapters of this book. The definitions and connotations may differ from what you generally are used to, or they may be exactly as you know them, but nonetheless we need align everyone's frame of reference so that the information transmits accurately.

Meditation is one of the most misunderstood disciplines in all of mankind's history. There are still websites out there that tout meditation as the ability to zero the mind and think of nothing. Others label meditation as the ability to chant, or attach it to religion. It is none of those things in any way or form.

Before we can look at what meditation is, we need to look at the source of meditation and the look at that source will give us an idea of what meditation is and what it is not. The foundation of meditation is mindfulness, and because it is a huge part of meditation, we are going to spend a major part of this book talking about mindfulness--what to expect when you get the practice right. Before you can do it, you need to know what it looks like when you stumble upon it.

Mindfulness

What is mindfulness? Here is another term that is loosely thrown around at every juncture to describe a number of things. Mindfulness is the ability to step back and watch everything going on around your mind without interacting with it and without judging it.

It is like standing at the side of the road and watching all the cars go by, without interacting with any of the cars. You observe, you accept and you let the flow of cars just remain as that. That is a simple picture of mindfulness.

Why would you do this? Why do you not interact with the flow of cars? The reason why you do not interact with the cars by stepping into its path is that your body isn't built to do it.

Steps to Practicing Mindfulness

These are the basics steps to introducing one's self to mindfulness. To do it, you have all you need. You don't need to buy anything or do anything. You are already doing it. Your breathing is your doorway to mindfulness. It is said that breathing is the anchor that connects the mind to the body. It is a simple phrase, but carries a tremendous amount of meaning, which will unfold to you as you become more accustomed to turning on your mindfulness at will.

Breathing is one of the most basic things that all human beings do. Regardless of shape, color, size, culture or religion, we all breathe. The most basic practice in attaining mindfulness is to watch your own breath without taking part in it. Try it. One proper way to watch your breath is to close your eyes and, without altering the cadence and rhythm of your breathing, just watch as your body inhales, pauses, exhales and pauses again - assuming your are in a state of rest. The critical point of this exercise is to differentiate the act of observing from the act of participating. Your first lesson in mindfulness is the importance of observing.

The act of observing is a very neutral function. Observing does not partake in the act. It does not react to the act - good, bad or indifferent. There is no reaction, not even the reaction of indifference. Of course, this takes a significant amount of practice, but as a child that we once were, we used to observe without an agenda and without a reaction. That is the essence of innocence. Innocence allows us to absorb our surrounding without judging and blocking. As you return to mindfulness, you will begin to experience this innocence as well.

Back to the example above - to be able to observe it, is to accept it as it is. If your cadence and rhythm are slow and deep, do not consciously make any effort to change it, define it or record it. The ultimate observation is to watch it in an unwavering manner. At this point in time, your breathing is controlled by the respiratory control center that is located at the base of the brain.

This simple act does a number of things. First, it calms you down and allows you to get comfortable. Second, it brings your attention inward and away from the chaos of the outside world. Third, it focuses your mind in a way that is enveloped in the wholeness of your breath.

But these are all outward effects of the mindfulness exercise. There is a deeper effect and ultimately, what we are in search of. More on that in the next chapter.

Chapter 2: Recognize The Mindful Teachers In Your Life

Once we can feel the difference between living alarmed and being mindful, we need help experiencing wellness more consistently. The short history of the mindfulness we practice today is the story of how to be well, passed from one teacher to the next.

Mindfulness is defined most simply as awareness or presence. It is the state of being wherever you are without judgment. As obvious as it sounds, it is not easy to make it your nature and habit all the time.

But regular mindfulness wasn't always so difficult. Our most ancient ancestors did not have apps or 783 television stations to sully their attention. They had the feeling of warm sun on a cold morning. They had the night sky and the chorus of the animals. They had the camp fire.

Then Buddha left his compound. As a child, Brahmins taught him to meditate. When nothing else brought him the answer to what would end all suffering, he sat under a tree. The traditions of intentionally sitting and breathing and the many exercises that came from that first sit began what today we call mindfulness. It was those first Brahmins who made the entire discipline possible.

Jump to 1966. The father of modern mindfulness discovered meditation. Jon Kabat-Zinn studied at MIT while the famed philosopher of religion Huston Smith introduced America to world religions including Buddhism. At 22, Kabat-Zinn began his practice. In the mid-seventies, he attended a conference with Thich Nhat Hanh. Kabat-Zinn had a realization: everyone, especially those suffering from chronic illness, can benefit from mindfulness.

In 1979 he began teaching an eight-week course at the Stress Reduction Clinic at

UMass Medical School in Worcester, Massachusetts. His purpose was to treat medical conditions like anxiety and depression by helping people drop into their bodies and be. Research on people who took the course literally found their brains changed. The alarm thinned. The parts of the brain responsible for memory, learning, and perspective thickened. Suddenly, the Western tradition of reason and science met the eternal power of not getting too caught up in the mind.

But without Smith and Hanh, Kabat-Zinn never would have begun the path that led mindfulness to be a scientifically validated medical intervention paid for by insurance. A guy with the initials JC was pretty prolific in his ability to be truly present; some say he learned from teachers in the East and certainly from a traveling mystic named John. Rumi knew the power of sitting and the orphic beauty of trees; his eyes were opened to the ascetic life by his accidental teacher, named Shams. We cannot learn the secrets of mindfulness without teachers.

What we have ignored in our busy lives is that people all around us are living differently. They don't see life as a race, even though they may be athletes. They don't try to prove they are right all the time, even though they may be freedom fighters and activists. What those who are mindful know that all of us need to practice is that each moment is the most precious gift we too often ignore. Even in the midst of suffering, there is stillness. Even in the midst of the best times, there is a profound quiet that outlasts the highs of success.

As mindfulness spread through the Western world, its watershed into mainstream culture happened on April 6, 2007. Media mogul Arianna Huffington, suffering from exhaustion, fainted and hit her head on the corner of her desk. The wake-up call kickstarted her focus on promoting mindfulness. Today, The

Huffington Post offers myriad mindfulness teachers from around the world a place to reach students. Oprah caught on and began advocating a 21-day meditation course with one of her gurus, Deepak Chopra. Mindfulness sections abound in every book store and meditative practices are taught in yoga classes, therapists' offices, and even schools around the world.

The wild fire of intentional presence continues to spread because mindfulness is better than living alarmed. But few of us can transition into being mindful more often without help. Who is the ancient teacher who most excites you? It could be a giant like the Buddha, JC, or Rumi. Who do you know who teaches mindfulness? It could be the yoga instructor down the street. It could be your friend who meditates.

Who is the person in your life who seems the most grounded and happy? Have you ever asked them how they do it? Those who can help us are everywhere if we look for them. Because they are mindful, they will deeply enjoy a conversation with you. The best news is that over time your brain can absolutely be as mindful as theirs.

Chapter 3: Setting Goals

It takes a lot more than a talent or a gift to rise to the top. Achieving success is no guesswork. You have to set the goals that you want to go for and then apply the effort until your goals come true. But simply because you have taken the step of setting goals doesn't automatically mean that they will materialize. There is a science to goal-setting and there are many facets you ought to factor in. One of the benefits of regularly practicing mindfulness is that we develop our capacity of setting goals and increase our odds of reaching them. The following are some of the ways that mindfulness promotes goal setting.

Sense of direction

Most talented people are afflicted with the inability of determining where they want their talent to take them. This is made clear when they start consuming anything on their path and put their hands on so many things. In order to set a reachable goal, you have to have a clear direction that you want to take. If you are not in touch with your inner self, it can be quite difficult to determine the most appropriate direction for you which can spell danger to your ambition. Being able to determine your direction correlates with your ability to perceive your strengths. You want to align yourself with the direction that feels natural to you. For instance, If you're a pretty woman, you have the body for both modeling and acting. In as much as you can get into both careers, there's one career that you stand to gain the most out of and you're the only person who can determine which career is that. Mindfulness empowers you to have a keen knowledge of yourself and you would know which field holds the most promise.

Foreseeing obstacles

The cleverest person is the one who has an idea of the challenges that wait in their future. If you are an imaginative person, it is not hard to conjure up these kinds of challenges. But if you just bulldoze around and set goals without giving a thought to future challenges, you leave yourself open to attacks and increase your chances of self-sabotage. The great thing about visualizing the obstacles that lie waiting in your future is that you can learn to do it. No rocket science in that. There are various mindfulness techniques that will develop your mind's capacity to view both the good and the bad of the future so that nothing catches you by surprise.

Our capacity to deal with temptations

There are distractions and then there are temptations. The obvious truth is that not many of us are equipped to handle temptations. For instance, we could hold very high offices and then at one point corruption rears its not-so-ugly head and we are tempted to take part in corruption at the expense of our goals. It takes a lot of commitment to be able to turn the other way in the face of a temptation. As you come at your goals, your resolve will be put to test more times than you will care to remember. But it is not okay to always fall sort of integrity. Practicing mindfulness on the regular fortifies your mind so that you are able to withstand the biggest temptation ever. And this is a big deal. An inability to handle temptation could set off your ruin.

Focusing on the most important stuff

Setting goals allow you to close in on the stuff that really matters. This arrangement quickens the process of transforming your goals into reality. When you are bogged down by trivial activities, you lose the energy that would have otherwise gone into the critical areas. For instance, if you are a business owner, when setting long-term goals for your business, some of the most important things will be customer retention, profits, and product delivery, whereas the not-so-important affairs will be things like your staff and corporate social responsibility. When you separate the important things from the not-so-important, you are in a position to hasten results by applying more effort into the most important stuff.

Decision making

An inability to make great decisions is what makes the difference between success and failure. Most people approach decision making as merely a toss-up. The stakes could be high, but still, the person has a cavalier attitude and ultimately this proves to be a costly mistake. Great decisions allow us to utilize resources to the greatest extent possible and to make use of all opportunities. Practicing mindfulness improves our critical thinking capacity which is a huge resource during decision-making. Studies show that decisions made based on realistic projections have a far better chance of coming to fruition than decisions that were born from delusions and unhinged fantasies.

Empowered to face the future

If there's one thing that the mind tends to be deeply wary of, it is uncertainty. And the mind responds to uncertainty with worry and anxiety. But when you convince your brain that you will reach your goals, the anxiety and worry will fritter away. In that sense, setting goals gives you control of your future.

Makes you more driven

Imagine yourself living as a free man and without any goals. You just wake up and go through the daily motions. Now imagine yourself with a proper set of long-term and short-term goals, as well as visual boards in your office as a reminder of where you want to be. Obviously, you are likely to be more driven and a self-starter in the second environment as opposed to the first. Setting goals flicks on your inherent motivation. You won't laze around watching cartoons when there's more important stuff that needs to be attended to. It is through mindfulness that we increase our capacity to set goals that are going to excite us to take action instead of boring us into a perpetual state of indolence.

Progress monitoring

It is not enough to set goals and expect everything to fall into place. You have to keep monitoring the progress of your goals in order to get rid of things that are likely to discourage the actualization of your goals. Through mindfulness, we get to improve our capacity to monitor our goals and hasten it all.

Chapter 4: Panic Attacks

When you're suffering from bouts of panic and anxiety, you'll most likely try to get some relief. You hate the way your life is taken over and you stop doing what you want... In fear of another attack, you're afraid to leave the house, and the fear of one evens increases the frequency. Your life gets out of control... how are you going to stop fits of panic and anxiety?

There's good news here... Panic treatment is available that not only helps to disperse the attacks, but also makes it possible to keep them from returning entirely.

Some doctors are still going to prescribe medications to ease the severity of your panic attacks, which also makes it difficult to feel any emotions. Drug treatment may make you feel like your head is surrounded by cotton wool, or any perception of life is now blurry, vague and clearly defined.

Many physicians are now promoting a new form of panic therapy that works very well, and people who don't want to rely on drugs are much preferred.

Since panic therapy does not use medication, you maintain a clear mind and are more able to recognize and avoid them when an anxiety or panic attack occurs. As there are causes for anxiety and panic attacks, it becomes easy enough to recognize them if you know what you are looking for. Such attacks are usually caused by stress, not just an occurrence, but also an accumulation of stress, likely over the years.

Everybody faces stress in their daily lives and most people can deal with it, but for some, it can only take' one more thing' and they are' overloaded' so the mind responds with fear or anxiety. The mind can then snowball into another after getting one, as the tension of expecting another attack in itself becomes a catalyst.

This turns into a vicious cycle, so breaking the cycle is the trick.

The good news is that behavioral therapy will help you recognize and look objectively at your causes and symptoms to help you get to where you can manage your emotions and anxiety. The other good thing about this therapy is that you're going from good to better as you make progress.

If you were taking medication, you would need to keep taking it to maintain the status quo and maybe even need to increase the dosage in order to have the same effect in some situations. In this case, it is possible to become quite dependent on these medications, and it can be difficult to get out of them, causing the panic attacks to re-surface, since they do not address the cause, only to suppress the symptoms.

Using this form of panic therapy is more likely to help you recover a normal lifestyle that helps you to cope with anything life brings. You will work at your speed through the counselling and do the job for you as you need it. This is critical, as no successful therapy can add stress to a stress-intensive situation.

Regardless of how intense the feelings were, it is possible to make sure and steady progress until the anxiety and panic attacks finally stop. It is important to remember that as it took time to build up to the point that panic attacks were triggered by stress, it will take time to decrease the frequency and intensity of the attacks before they cease to occur.

Panic Attacks: The Mindfulness Therapy Approach to Anxiety

Panic attacks and panic disorder are affecting an increasing number of people in the United States and Western Europe. It's hard to understand how unbearably painful panic anxiety is for those who experience ongoing panic attacks for those who don't suffer from panic attacks. The experience is very vivid for the victims of panic disorder; it is a full-blown fight or flight style response that can cause dramatic increases in heart rate and trigger profuse sweating and many other changes in physiology and biochemistry. Imagine walking along a trail and unexpectedly meeting a mountain lion; that's how it feels-and sometimes much worse-for those with panic anxiety.

Panic anxiety is not just "in the mind" as some may believe, but it comes from an integrated reaction involving both mind and body; both helping the reactive cycle. Essentially, though, it is what happens in the mind that causes the mental and physiological processes leading to a full-blown panic attack. Many patients with panic anxiety are looking for ways to change the underlying mental process that causes anxiety. Some resort to some sort of counselling or talk therapy, others choose a more straightforward therapeutic approach like CBT or Mindfulness Therapy as they try to change the internal mechanism that causes the emotional reaction that then activates the body reactions.

At the root of panic disorders, you can eventually find some form of reactive thinking that causes panic attacks, and the idea behind CBT is, of course, that if you can alter these normal habits of negative thinking and negative attitudes you will disperse the panic attacks. They take this a step further in the Mindfulness Therapy approach, as they understand that the concern is not just with the substance of the thoughts or values or memories, but with the emotional energy that is absorbed into these specific modes of thought. It is this emotional charge that gives negative thoughts, convictions, or traumatic memories of some control. That's why two people can think the same thoughts but react quite differently- because different people have different emotional charges. Through Mindfulness Therapy, therefore, the focus is on finding ways to change this emotional energy, allowing it to discharge itself and overcome itself. Then all that remains is an "empty image" that stops having any specific meaning or power to cause anxiety or misery.

Clients/students learn to "rest" with their feelings in mindfulness therapy. It means that with anger, resistance or denial they learn to keep the emotion in their conscious awareness without getting lost in the narrative of becoming sensitive to the emotion. This fundamental change in relationship from being overwhelmed by an emotion to being able to observe the emotion as an entity that is central to our consciousness. In Mindfulness Therapy, we call this the primary relationship, and this provides the best possible conditions in which the emotional charge can begin to discharge itself. Then negative thoughts and beliefs start losing their strength and losing their control over you.

During the day, find a quiet time and practice sitting with your fear of panic. During a panic attack, it's hard to do this, but it's quite possible to do it when you're not. How you learn to do is meditate on the emotion itself, making it the object of conscious awareness. In this deliberate manner, you will begin to develop a relationship with the emotion itself, not based on reactivity, which only reinforces the issue, but on consciousness, which provides the perfect inner atmosphere for transformation. You start breaking free from the usual patterns of reactivity, becoming stronger and more balanced by repeatedly returning to the emotion and cultivating this non-reactive relationship. But, more than that, this meditation on the emotion's consciousness creates the inner space where the emotion begins to change and transform itself.

Get Rid Of Panic Attacks for Good

Anxiety self-help tips are everywhere, believe it or not, some are going to work, some are not going to work depending on who you are and the severity of your anxiety. However, you can almost make sure you can substantially reduce the amount of anxiety you experience by embracing and performing some of these tips.

And what are some of the signs when coping with anxiety that people experience? Believe it or not, there are almost unlimited amounts of symptoms, such as dry mouth and rapid heartbeats-sweating, heavy breathing, claustrophobia, the sensation that everything appears unreal, or out of control. There's also a lot of others, and by finding out what the signs are and connecting them to anxiety, you'll also be able to know what causes them.

So here's one thing you can do to get rid once and for all of this fear. You want to make sure you avoid the anxiety or panic attacks inducing climate. When you can't do this, you'd like to make a dietary change. Drinking tons of heavy caffeine items like many energy drinks, coffee, and sodas will help the body's anxiety and tension-caffeine is a stimulant and can be attributed to many panic attacks occurring.

To get rid of these panic attacks once and for all, another thing you can do is try massage therapy. There are techniques for self-massage, but even a massage parlor can be found to help you get in and relax your body. Try the techniques of deep breathing, aromatherapy, and meditation. Ultimately, you can relax your mind and body and try to reduce your anxiety!

The Complete Fundamental Basics to Eliminating Panic Attacks for Good

A panic attack is a sudden anxiety that happens without warning. It can happen to anybody irrespective of race, age or gender. Recognizing the signs of an attack is crucial and understanding how to stop an attack from there.

It is necessary to know the signs and symptoms before learning how to avoid a panic attack. One of the many signs of an attack is panic, a "racing heart," chest tightness, stomach pain, dizziness, breathing difficulties, and hot flashes. Those who had witnessed such a situation said they felt insane and mistaken it for a heart attack.

It can be simple to stop a panic attack, but it must be done immediately. One of the first steps is to accept an attack and relax. To calm down, take in long, deep breaths and drink plenty of water.

Trying to stop the flow of negative thoughts and thinking positive is also crucial, reminding yourself that you are going to get through this. Pressure yourself or call a friend to focus on something else like a TV show. The expressed thoughts that triggered the attack will subside by keeping your mind occupied with other activities.

Panic attacks typically last less than 10 minutes, though they may last longer in some situations. After suffering from an assault, when the next incident happens, one might start worrying and obsessive. Because such attacks are caused by fear, fear will only create a vicious cycle that will trigger another attack.

Understanding the root cause of the attacks is the most effective way to stop a panic attack. You can do that by talking to a therapist, who will help you find the negative cause and replace it with more positive and realistic thoughts. You may be able to overcome the attacks by understanding your fear.

Coping With Panic Attacks Using Mindfulness Meditation

If at the moment you're not coping very well with panic attacks and you'd like to change that as soon as possible, one of the best things you can do for yourself is to start practicing meditation with carefulness. This is a much-underused approach to dealing with the symptoms and issues that can cause severe panic and anxiety disorders, and that's a shame as it provides amazing results for a significant proportion of the people who seek it.

If this approach is for you a brand new concept, let's take a quick look at exactly what it is and what it entails.

Mediation of mindfulness is the concentrated consciousness of your emotions, intentions, and behavior. It allows us to remain fully focused on the present moment and helps us to avoid being distracted by the unpredictable and often uncontrollable thoughts that pop up throughout the day in our minds.

We can take a step back from our thoughts and the internal commentary in our minds by learning to live only in the present moment. Our emotions no longer have control over us when we reach this state we know that they are just thoughts, and we are better able to let them go.

Partitioning meditation for mindfulness is a great first step if you don't deal with panic attacks.

Explaining what knowledge is and how to use it in your own life with you here is beyond the reach of my time, but luckily some many excellent books and websites explain the process. If you think this may help your situation, then I encourage you to take a closer look at your sensitivity and try to incorporate it into your everyday life.

Anxiety Attack Vs. Attack Panic-Are These the Same

While many believe that anxiety attacks and panic attacks are the same as clinical outlook, they are not. The American Psychiatric Association's Diagnostic and Statistical Manual of Mental Disorders (Abbreviation: DSM) has defined the term panic disorders, but DSM does not explicitly describe anxiety disorders. Alternatively, under anxiety, some disorders falling under anxiety are cited.

The main distinctions between these two attacks are explained below: The major difference between an anxiety attack and a panic attack is the attack's severity and duration. In the former case, relative to panic disorders, the severity is lower. There are many common symptoms between those two types of attack such as dizziness, nausea, elevated heart bit rate, agitation, etc., but in contrast with an anxiety attack, the severity is nowhere near panic attacks. Anxiety attacks also last longer, generally about 45 minutes. At the same time, in most situations, panic attacks last about 10 to 15 minutes.

Attacks of anxiety are often influenced by a stressor. Suppose you're walking down a dark alley with no other passer-by. Suddenly, nearby you hear a footstep and then an anxiety attack can be made. Panic attacks, however, do not involve a stressor. These are mostly spontaneous and can occur without proper reason (that being said, long periods of stress in a human being can cause panic attacks). A person is seized with fear and terror in the event of panic attacks. He also begins to feel acute pain in certain parts of the body. He thinks he's going to die or have a heart attack that increases the multiplicity of fears.

It follows anticipatory anxiety with attacks. If you get a panic attack, your mind is always swallowed up by the anxiety that another will soon suffer. Instead of talking about how to handle panic attacks, people get obsessed with the attack and its effects. Anxiety attacks can take place over a certain period, however, and if healed completely with the help of a professional, there is a thin chance that it will return.

When a person gets a panic disorder at some point, in any future he starts to avoid the same location. In case of an anxiety attack, though, the same does not happen.

No matter how many similarities these two may have, it requires serious attention to both of these assaults. Perhaps, a professional visit is what you need to resolve both.

Chapter 5: Examples Of Mindfulness In Your Life

How often have you sipped a drink or eaten a sandwich and not really noticed what it tasted like? Life, in general, is a rush and the millennial generation can truly testify to this. When we rush our food or drink – basic processes we all need to do, every day of our lives to survive – we don't give the digestive system the attention it merits, yet we all have the potential to do this easily. Hang on, are you inferring you can eat or drink, mindfully? Yep, sure am! Let's take you back to the good ol' days in your highchair when your parents decided it was time for an introduction to solid foods. Ok, so you probably don't actually remember that far back. Let me open that one from the archives for you. When you were handed your first ever piece of watermelon, remember the sweet smell of those innocent looking little pink cubes? The sticky wet sensation as you (to the frustration of your parents) crushed little pieces of it between your fingers and palm, and the squelching noise that came with it? The taste as it tore between your teeth and turned into mush before you swallowed?

You paid attention to all of your senses in your experience. You were completely invested in that moment of learning. You were, in your glorious infancy of babyhood, mindful!

If you'd like to look at a more adult example, take a basic task such as making a home brewed coffee. Listen to the noise of the coffee maker and smell the aroma as it wafts across the room. Sit down somewhere comfortable with minimal distraction and hold the warm mug between your hands. Again, perhaps a little visualization of holding your mug in a cozy armchair in front of a fire in a wood cabin might help to engage at the moment.

When you eat and drink mindfully, meaning you sit down and consciously give your attention to the process and responses of your senses, you are practicing a very basic and yet also very effective technique of training yourself to be invested at the moment. You also inadvertently benefit your digestive system by slowly consuming your food, and there are now various studies and books available on the links between mind and gut health I strongly suggest you look into.

In comparison, when you don't eat mindfully, you risk causing digestive issues, and you cannot invest at the moment – you're simply treating the process as a chore, and you fail to engage your senses in response. You may also find productivity falls while you continue in a rush and do not take the time to refocus.

Handling Negative Emotions

Negative emotions are part and parcel of life, but how often do you encounter a negative emotion and consciously decide, before that emotion really takes hold, "how long do I want to feel this way?" Probably not often!

And yet, this is another example of something really basic you can practice every day on your journey to becoming a more mindful person. When you apply a mindful approach in this context, you simply empty your mind of negativity; mellow the thought and neutralize it of all judgement. Judgement is self-defeating, in that you are trying to put things in some sort of order that doesn't realistically represent the situation, and trying to make sense of that order goes on to snowball.

It might sound a little cliché, but I'm going to say it: Everything happens for a reason. In saying that, you must be careful not to over-analyze the phrase to the extent it upsets you and prompts a negative emotional cycle. What I mean is, when you approach changes and events (small daily scenarios or life-changing circumstances) with a degree of acceptance, you enable gratitude which prompts a positive cycle of experiencing potentially negative feelings that may give rise to positive outcomes. You discover a moral in each of your stories. Once you become attuned to the idea of identifying a positive outcome from a negative situation, you soon discover a new lease on life and greater self-awareness.

Spoiler Alert: Bestselling author Elizabeth Gilbert's memoir, Eat, Pray, Love, is a powerful story and perfect example of overcoming negativity to achieve mindfulness and emotional independence. Following a difficult split with her ex-husband, she proceeds to go on a journey to learn meditation. However, thoughts of her ex-husband and their relationship constantly inhibit her journey, and for as long as she insisted on holding onto the negative connotations of that relationship, she could not succeed at meditation. When she successfully gains control of her thought patterns and finds acceptance for what she has experienced and the events that followed (a realization in how negative circumstances eventuated to positive outcomes), she is able to acknowledge her life without regret and accept what has happened – she unlocks a self-awareness that puts her back in control. There is a wonderful acceptance knowing that one moment flows into the next and change happens regardless of how much we might initially resist.

Ridding Negative Thoughts

Bluntly put, you cannot rid yourself of all negative thoughts, and it's too idealistic to think you can. For example, the loss of a loved one requires a grieving process that may not initially allow acceptance for some time, and that is perfectly normal. You need to grieve and should allow yourself as much time as you need. While you may not have control over acceptance in some situations, you do have control over how you want those thoughts to proceed at that moment. Again, ask yourself, "how long do I want to feel this way?"

For example, in a situation where someone is angry, often heated words are exchanged that are regrettable the moment we finish the sentence. Rather than becoming your anger, use mindfulness to create a space between yourself and your anger – consider your anger almost like a separate person – it's up to you whether you want to interact with them or not, and maintaining your sense of calm in the face of anger will quickly negate the need for it to exist. You may also find you have something to gain from the situation rather than losing from it, and implementing practices such as your breathing techniques can prevent negative thoughts from causing a chain-reaction of negativity.

Mindful Waking

How we start the day can play a huge part in how the day unfolds. "Did you get up on the wrong side of the bed this morning?" is likely something we have all asked someone before, or been asked ourselves. For others, we're a complete wreck without our morning coffee. It's common routine to wake to the sound of an alarm that drones "work!" or "kids to school!" and we're immediately frustrated or rushed. Instead of leaving the alarm until the last minute (no pun intended), set your alarm a few minutes earlier so you can practice mindful waking. Get out of bed and look out your window – draw back the curtains or pull up the blind and breathe in the air of a new day. Acknowledge something basic you can see like a bird sitting on a fence, and dedicate your observation for that moment to the bird – acknowledge and appreciate the gift of nature embodied in the bird's visit to you. When you feel calm and ready, draw your attention away from the moment and kickstart your productivity by making the bed and commencing your day. Mindful waking is just another basic example of introducing mindfulness into your daily routine to improve your approach to life. The next chapter will explain how mindfulness can evolve the spiritual side of your nature. However, this doesn't have anything to do with religion. Rather, it concerns the balance that you create between yourself and the world around you, and your acceptance of all the gifts of life through mindful thought and practice.

Chapter 6: The History Of Mindfulness

Mindfulness is basically a practice that is involved in different secular and religious traditions – from Buddhism and Hinduism to yoga and even the non-religious meditations that have come in practice today. People have practiced mindfulness for a thousand years; it does not matter whether it is on its own or maybe as part of the larger tradition. Much just like yoga, the history of mindfulness and meditation is spiritual and ancient but originated in religion. It is important to note that mediation even predates the ancient times, having its origins in the old religions that included rhythmic mantras or chants. However, the earliest records for meditation can still be found in the oldest text of the Hinduism that is known as Vedas. It dates from 1700 to 1100 BCE, which is several years ago. As time moved by, various forms of meditation would be introduced in Taoism and Buddhism, particularly in China and India. The main focus of the ancient meditation appeared to be on transcending emotions and spiritual growth to coexist in a surrounding that calm and safe. Having been introduced to the western market in the 20th century, meditation was then realigned to match the main goals of a secular and modern society. It did not take time before it was used as a way of lowering stress and improving the general health of all human beings. In fact, it is the female version of yoga.

Mindfulness was popularized in the East by a team of spiritual and religious institutions, whereas in the West its popularity draws its roots to certain secular institutions and a certain group of people. As a matter of fact, even the secular tradition of mindfulness in the western region owes its roots to the Eastern traditions and religions.

Having pointed out that, a number of modern Western teachers and practitioners of mindfulness learned about mindfulness in the Hindu and Buddhist tradition. In a nutshell, it is important to note that mindfulness meditation has been practiced for thousands of years. Its main origins are from the Eastern philosophy, and over the past forty years, the practice has been so much in the western cultures. Mindfulness has its origin in ancient meditation practices.

Jon Kabat-Zinn is the foundation that started the Stress Reduction Clinic, which is based at the University of Massachusetts Medical School. This happened in the late 1970s. Form that time, close to 20,000 have successfully finished up the MBSR program that has been siting with certain conditions like sleep process, heart diseases, chronic pain, psoriasis, anxiety, and depression.

In the year 1990, a group of three people came up with MBSR for the sole purpose of offering assistance to those who had depression-related issues. The three individuals were Zindel Seagul, John Teasdale, and Mark Williams. It was at the same period that MBCT – Mindfulness-Based Cognitive Therapy combined CBT with Mindfulness to offer the best. At the moment, MBCT is clinically approved by the NICE- National Institute for the Clinical Excellence. This is a treatment of choice for those who have recurring depression.

The history of mindfulness can also be traced back to the historical practice and religion. It actually started in 1500 BCE in the Hinduism culture under the main context of yoga. Daoism was in existence since the 6th c. BCE in the context of the qi gong exercise.

On the other hand, Buddhism began in 535 BCE in the whole context of focusing on breath patterns. Besides those cultures, it was also found in Jewish, Muslim, and Christian practices. As of now, the practice has been widely applied in the psychology field to assist those who have personality disorders, pain, anxiety, and depression. The main reason why mindfulness was studied was to see the effectiveness of restlessness, emotion, and cognition on people. This is according to the research work that was undertaken by the Centre for Mindfulness Research and Practice in the year 2015.

As a matter of fact, the interest of a number of psychologists in this field grew when the stress reduction clinic started offering evidence for the role that meditation played on the regulation of emotion. Other additional research was carried out, and before long, it became one of the leading methodologies applied by practitioners to assist clients attain the metacognitive awareness. This is the awareness of the thought process.

The result of applying mindfulness, in either religion or scientific form is just calmness. The main aim of both forms is to assist deal with the restless thoughts, emotional aspects, and it will also, in return, make you a more compassionate person and aware of your current environment. However, the Buddhist mindfulness also promises you with just similar wisdom as the original idea of mindfulness.

The cultivation of mindfulness, on its own side, has its main roots in Buddhism, even though most of the religions include certain kinds of prayer meditating methodologies that assist in shifting your thoughts away from the normal preoccupation toward an appreciation of the moment and an extended perspective of life.

It is the professor emeritus Jon Kabat-Zinn, the former director and founder of the Stress Reduction Clinic at the University of Massachusetts Medical Center, who assisted to introduce mindfulness meditation practice into mainstream medicine. He also went ahead to demonstrate that practicing mindfulness could introduce improvements in both the psychological and physical symptoms as well as the positive changes in the health behaviors and attitudes. Professor Kabat-Zinn was introduced to the Buddhism philosophy for the first time when he was a student at MIT.

He would later start the Stress Reduction Clinic in 1979 at the University of Massachusetts Medical School. While here, he adapted the teachings of Buddhists on mindfulness and created the MBSR – Mindfulness-Based Stress Reduction. He later gave the program another name – MBSR – getting rid of the framework of Buddhism and then downplayed any connection that is between Buddhism and mindfulness, as opposed to putting MBSR in a more scientific context. To this date, Professor Kabat-Zinn downplays the connection that is between Buddhism and mindfulness.

In the year 2013, Kabat-Zinn gave the definition of mindfulness as the psychological process of incorporating one's attention to both the external and internal experiences taking place in the current moment – and this can be developed through the practice of meditation among a number of other trainings. According to a piece of information that was later provided by Robert Sharf, the Buddhist word that was translated into English as mindfulness came from the Pali term sati, and smrti, its Sanskrit counterpart.

The original meaning of the word Smrti was to bear in mind, to recollect, or to remember. It is basically an awareness of things in relation to some other things, thus creating awareness of their specific value. It is essential to remember that Sati is what makes the yoga practitioner remember that any kind of feeling that they might undergo takes place in its relation to an entire variety of feelings that may be either unskillful or skillful, faultless or with faults, refined or relative inferior, and pure or dark.

The Relationship Between Mindfulness and Religion

If the above understating of Sati is compared to another understanding, the definition of mindfulness from the perspective of Kabat-Zinn, the influence of Buddhism is found in the thoughts of Kabat-Zinn. Kabat-Zinn gives the description of mindfulness, as a way of paying attention in a given manner; on purpose, or in the current moment, but in a manner that is entirely non-judgmental. Recent interest has come up for studying the main effects of mindfulness on the brain through the application of the techniques of neuroimaging, behavioral tests, and a number of other physiological measures. According to a recent research that was undertaken at Harvard University, the brain is able to develop new gray matter through the process of meditation, which is a mainstay of mindfulness.

When the density of the gray matter is high in the hippocampus, which is known to be very instrumental for memory and learning, as well as in the structure that is linked to introspection, compassion, and self-awareness were discovered in this particular study. It is even very interesting to see the plasticity of the brain, and the fact that, by practicing meditation, we are in apposition to perform a very integral role in changing the brain and can still increase the quality of life and our well being. This is according to Britta Holzel, who was a research fellow at Giessen University and MGH in Germany. He went ahead to note that other studies in various patient populations have proved that meditation can create great improvements in a number of symptoms, and the underlying mechanisms in the brain that facilitate this particular change have not been investigated.

The Harvard study is just one among the many studies that have discussed the whole topic of mindfulness as well as its effectiveness when it comes to clinical settings. Apart from just proving efficacy, research data also plays another important role in showing that mindfulness is not really a fad. Several centuries ago, Buddhists fully comprehended the transforming power of the whole topic of mindfulness. As things stand right now, we can confidently confirm that the Buddhists were actually very right.

Modern mindfulness has been able to penetrate through the entire western culture will every person from the corporate firms, sporting teams, schools and even movie actors citing it as a very important tool for success. As noted in this chapter, mindfulness has a rich history. They include meditation practices, yoga, Buddhism, and Hinduism. All these practices have the same goals in training one's attention and assist in calming the mind. As it's been its main essence, mindfulness just means paying attention, purposefully for the present moment, with certain underlying qualities that include acceptance, curiosity, and compassion. This promotes a nice means of living of focusing on the current moment as opposed to just dwelling on past events or worrying so much about the future.

People, typically, associate mindfulness with Buddhism even though there is a group of commentators who have argued that the history of mindfulness should never be reduced to Buddhism. As noted earlier, mindfulness shares some roots from Hinduism, Islam, Christianity, and Judaism. It is also very clear that there are some religions that posses an aspect of mindfulness and it is universally accepted that Buddhism and Hinduism are the leading religions where mindfulness has stemmed from.

The practice of mindfulness creates an important part of Buddhist teachings since around 400 to 500 B.C.E. As a matter of fact, the Buddha himself made reference to it as the main path to enlightenment. Therefore, 2,600 years since that time, many who have followed in the footsteps of Buddha have upheld his mindfulness practices and teachings. In the context of Buddhism, mindfulness meditation serves three main roles, including

Identifying the mind

Training the mind, as well as

Freeing the mind

It is the unity that exists between breath, mind, and body that links both mindfulness and yoga together. Yoga is, in fact, a Sanskrit word that means unity.

Both yoga and mindfulness have several crossovers particularly in regards to body awareness. In yoga, the body is used to connect to oneself, and the body scan might similarly be used to be aware of the kind of sensations that are present in the body, each time we pay attention to our bodies via the postures, or asana, as they are called, we apply it as a tool of becoming forever present.

Whereas it is just fair to point out that Buddhism has just made the most robust application of the methodology for purposes of enhancing mindfulness, secular mindfulness still uses meditation to cultivate mindfulness without actually relying on the doctrines provided by a number of spiritual traditions such as Buddhism. This makes the power of mindfulness to be available to a large number of people, including even the practitioners of various religions or none entirely.

The History of Mindfulness in Summary

Teachings of the Buddha were first recorded in the 5th century BC. They would later be passed for more than 450 years. The main Buddhist canons during this period were Vajrayana, Theravada,

and Mahayana. Vajrayana served the following areas;
- Russia
- Bhutan
- India
- Nepal
- Mongolia
- Tibet

The second one serves areas such as Laos, India, Cambodia, Thailand, Sri Lanka and other areas. Mahayana, on the other hand, served Korea, Vietnam, Japan, and China. The western schools of traditional Buddhism were also divided in various areas such as therapeutic mindfulness (MBSR, MBCT), Buddhist Psychology of The West, as well as the Secular Buddhism.

Chapter 7: Benefits Of Mindfulness

Without any doubt, there are many benefits that can be derived from becoming a regular practitioner of mindfulness as a whole concept. Let's start with the fact that both your mental and physical health is going to be improved. Numerous studies have demonstrated that mindfulness can help people fight against symptoms of depression, anxiety and obsessive-compulsive disorders. Mindfulness can help with substance abuse, eating disorders such as anorexia or bulimia or it can bring couples closer together, helping them solve existing conflicts.

When it comes to physical health, studies performed on people with different medication conditions have revealed that mindfulness has a positive impact when it comes to relieving stress, reducing the risks associated with cardiovascular diseases or lowering the blood pressure. The regular practice of mindfulness can help by reducing chronic pain, eliminating abnormal sleep patterns or even alleviating the symptoms of different gastrointestinal disorders.

Perhaps one of the most important things that you have to remember about mindfulness is that it teaches you to concentrate on the present, accepting the things that are happening without making any judgment. Why do you need to remember that? The answer is simple and quite obvious. Mindfulness will help you be more satisfied with your life and discover what happiness is all about, but only if you learn to concentrate on the present and accept things without judgment or placing labels. The more you practice mindfulness, the easier it will be to enjoy the good things you have in your life; you will learn how to fully immerse yourself in the present, finding the necessary energy to fight with negative situations.

As mindfulness is all about concentrating on the present, one of the biggest benefits will be the fact that you will learn how to let go of the worries. You will no longer waste important time and energy worrying about what happened in the past or what will happen in the future. Being more anchored in the present, you will be able to connect to other people and form relationships that extend to deeper and more intimate levels. Mindfulness will become a natural thing that is part of you, as it will help you to accept any experience (including pain or negative emotions) without judgment. Often times, our first reactions to negative situations are either in the form of aversion or avoidance. By practicing mindfulness, you will have better control over the processing of pain and negative emotions, handling such situations in a more efficient manner.

Mindfulness has been demonstrated to contribute to the reduction of rumination, which ultimately leads to the elimination of depression symptoms. Those who have practiced mindfulness and meditation have been known to have a better working memory, with increased concentration and better academic performance (reflected in their grades and academic assignments). Mindfulness allows one to concentrate on the present but it also teaches another important thing and that is how to suppress the information that is not useful or distracting. In regard to the processing of emotions, more recent studies have shown that the constant practice of mindfulness allows people to disengage more easily from things that are emotionally upsetting.

Regular practitioners of mindfulness have improved cognitive functions, demonstrating cognitive flexibility at the same time. Through a series of mindfulness exercises, they develop self-observation skills and they discover the best responses to a situation that is either negative or stressful. Also, mindfulness has been shown to increase the satisfaction within a relationship. Couples who practice mindfulness and meditation deal better with the common stress that any relationship includes; plus, they learn how to communicate their emotions to their partners in a more efficient manner.

Mindfulness works on different levels, allowing a person to become more aware of the inner self, to reach a new moral ground, to have better intuition and handle fear and other negative emotions. It can help one discover the true self, guaranteeing the discovery of the blind spots (accentuate or reduce the existence of a certain defect). A study performed on a controlled group also demonstrated mindfulness to improve the functioning of the immune system. Other studies performed on army employees have demonstrated that not only does mindfulness reduce the psychological distress but it also promotes a better recovery after stressful situations (war-related and not only). Army employees who have practiced meditation on a regular basis also had better performance in the workplace.

As mindfulness improves the cognitive functions of the brain, it should come as no surprise that regular practitioners process the information at a faster speed. Moreover, they handle different tasks in a more efficient manner and they can concentrate on a given task, without their minds wandering to other thoughts. Newer studies performed on older people have demonstrated that mindfulness protects against neurodegenerative conditions, by increasing the signaling connections in the brain. Practically, it keeps the brain young and focused, which is more than desirable in today's hectic world.

Chapter 8: The Physical Benefits Of Meditation

Here we are going to look at some of the physical benefits in detail and why the claims are being made.

Longevity

If you pay attention to the media, then you may well be aware of the natural antioxidant called resveratrol. Many academic research papers have been conducted on resveratrol, more than 220,000 in fact. What this research shows, is just how good resveratrol is at anti-ageing. It's been shown to improve our memory, inhibit cancer and vascular disease, prevent Alzheimer's and dementia, lower cholesterol and repair damage done by free radicals. In short, it is a bit of a wonder.

It achieves its impressive age-prevention properties by acting in two ways. Firstly, as a powerful antioxidant and secondly by activating specific gene proteins called "sirtuins." So powerful are the properties of sirtuins, that they have been researched heavily by pharmaceutical companies trying to isolate their anti-aging properties, specifically SIRT1 as it has been shown to increase cell survival rates. Unfortunately for the pharmaceutical companies, bottling this has proved exceedingly difficult.

The great news is that you can activate your sirtuins in better ways than downing a handful of expensive pills. Drinking red wine is one way, but much more excitingly so is practicing meditation. In fact, meditation can boost your SIRT1 by 52%, as shown in a study conducted in 2017. Over a 12-week period, six meditators were assessed for specific metabotropic cellular aging biomarkers. It was discovered that sirtuin 1 levels were significantly boosted by 52%. So, if you want a long-life meditation seems to be one way to help you achieve it.

Resveratrol and the sirtuins they activate are not the end of the story when it comes to meditation and longevity. Another important anti-aging chemical – Nitric Oxide essential for the healthy function of our immune system, brain, lungs, liver, pancreas and arteries. Is significantly boosted by regular meditation. It regulates blood pressure, is bacteria killing antioxidant, relays information between our nerves and cells, dilated the blood vessels, activates male erection, and more besides.

It was previously thought that the best way to promote a significant increase in nitric oxide levels was through stringent calorie restriction. But in 2007, 88 Tibetans had their blood tested by researchers from the US. They found that these Tibetans had 1000% more nitric oxide present in their blood than normal. It was argued that apart from meditation, the high altitude could also have a significant effect on the findings. So, another study was done by Ohio State University in 2014. It was conducted on a group of amateur meditators, practicing at regular altitudes. They were still shown to have a 213% increase in nitric oxide.

But the benefits of meditation and the key to longevity don't even stop there. Meditation lengthens Telomeres. Telomeres are rather like protective caps at the end of each strand of your DNA. They shield our chromosomes from damage, rather like those little plastic ends on shoelaces that prevent them from fraying.

Our DNA is the genetic material that makes up all the cells in our bodies. It makes us who we are. Every part of us is made up of cells ordered by our DNA.

In order to regenerate, cells copy themselves. This process happens continually throughout our entire lives. Each time a cell is copied the telomeres get shortened until eventually, they get too short to protect the DNA from damage which in turn creates damaged cells.

But it isn't only age that shortens our telomeres, stress, poor diet, lack of exercise, obesity and smoking also have significant effect.

Scientists from the University of California-Davis discovered that people who meditate had white blood cells with significantly longer and stronger telomeres than a control group. The reason for this it is thought is again down to stress reduction.

Skin Anti-Ageing

Another gene affected by meditation is NF-kB. This gene is responsible for accelerating skin ageing. Scientific studies have shown that rather than activating this gene meditation deactivates it. NF-kB causes chronic inflammation. It is activated by many of the regular suspects processed sugar, poor diet, insufficient sleep, smoking, sunlight, environmental toxins and the biggest of all, stress. It is the way that meditation significantly lowers our stress levels by reducing cortisol and altering our brain's fear response that it also switches off our NF-kB gene.

Pain and Illness

People suffering chronic pain often have to learn to simply live with it. Meditation has been shown to have significant effects on reducing pain and it does so in a number of ways:

Meditation changes the neural pathways within the brain. It can essentially override the pain thought process. MRI scans of 18 chronic pain sufferers, were done for a study conducted by Wake Forest University in 2011. After just 4 days of meditation, the pain centers in their brains were 57% less active.

Stress, causes our brain to release cortisol. This in turn increase inflammation, raises blood pressure, elevates heart rate and can significantly impact pain. Meditation lowers stress and reduces cortisol release, thus reducing pain.

When experiencing pain most of us reach for the painkillers sitting in our bathroom cabinet. The problem with this is that those drugs come with a range of nasty side effects. They damage our body, can create dependency and even addiction, they numb our senses and merely mask the problem rather than fixing it. Meditation works in a totally different way; it releases endorphins. These are our body's natural pain killers. They have no side effects and stimulate our bodies own natural healing ability.

Immune System. Not only will meditation help us with pain relief, but it also gives our immune system a massive boost. Stress and lowered immunity go hand in hand.

There is an interesting example of a Dutch man called Wim Hof or "The Iceman." Through meditation, he trained his body to withstand extreme subzero temperatures. But scientists also injected him with bacteria that causes flu-like symptoms. To which he had absolutely no response. Showing his immune system was exceedingly efficient.

At the University of Wisconsin-Madison, a study was conducted on 25 healthy employees. They practiced mindfulness meditation for 8 weeks. The study discovered that meditation activated an important area of the brain that is linked to the functioning of the immune system. It also showed a powerful antibody response when the participants were given the flu vaccine.

T Cells and Antibodies are also boosted by meditation improving our immune system. T cells and antibodies work as your body's defense system. They are like soldiers defending us from threats made upon it by viruses, bacteria and germs. The true power of this has been show in medical studies done on people with AIDS. One such study conducted by the University of California at Los Angeles (UCLA), was done on 50 HIV positive men. The study found with only 30 to 45 minutes of mindfulness meditation a day that the decline of their CD4 T cells, which are normally destroyed by the virus, was dramatically reduced. In some cases, meditation even helped to stop the disease's progression altogether.

Headaches. Research conducted by Herbert Benson MD, Helen P. Klemchuck AB and John R Graham MD found that the regular practice of meditation can help to reduce headaches by 37% or more. The study also showed that some forms of meditation completely eliminated headaches altogether in some people.

Headaches have a number of causes, one of them being body tension, especially when found in the face, jaw and neck. As meditation relaxes the entire body, it naturally alleviates this problem, thus reducing headaches.

Brain

Meditation has been seen to cause many amazing effects on the brain. The brainwave patterns from someone with an unhealthy, unbalanced brain, show that the two hemispheres of the brain are unbalanced. One side is used more than the other. They do not work together in sync.

The left-brain hemisphere is responsible for logical, mathematical, scientific and practical thinking. While the right brain hemisphere is responsible for intuitive, creative, abstract thinking. By using meditation, brainwaves can be transformed, allowing them to become balanced. This allows the brain to reorganize and create new neural pathways. The two hemispheres can then be seen to work and communicate together. This is known as "whole brain synchronization."

The benefits gained by whole brain synchronization include a significant increase in its ability to strengthen and grow. It increases the brains neuroplasticity. This means your mind is awakened, enabling you to be more focused and deep thinking. It will improve your memory, intellect, cognitive performance and overall mental health. It makes us happier with few feelings of anxiety, anger, depression or addiction. The more meditation is done, the more these effects become apparent. The evidence for this is backed by 1000s of different studies conducted by neuroscientists.

Hormones & Chemicals

Many of our body's hormones and other important chemicals are directly affected by meditation.

Growth Hormone. After puberty, this hormone is responsible for keeping your body tissues strong, healthy and young.

Melatonin. Responsible for sleep, but also for regulating women's menstrual cycles, stimulating white blood cell production, helping people with attention deficit-hyperactivity disorder (ADHD) and attention deficit disorder (ADD). It also minimizes bone loss and can help in the prevention and treatment of some cancers, depression, IBS and more.

Dehydroepiandrosterone. This is better known as DHEA and sometimes called the "longevity molecule." It counteracts the effects of stress. As you age, so does your DHEA level, but meditation can have a significant counter effect on this. It helps you alleviate depression, aids weight loss, normalizes adrenal function, improves sex function and libido, slows brain aging, slows HIV progression, combats diabetes, improves some cancers, prevents insulin resistance, lowers cholesterol, and has beneficial effects on lupus, eczema, asthma, hives and pneumonia.

Serotonin and Gamma Aminobutyric Acid (GABA). If we are low on these brain chemicals, then we become vulnerable to stress, anxiety and depression. Taking anti-anxiety and depression medication is not good. It leaves you feeling like a zombie; it can cause drowsiness, memory loss, confusion, dizziness, poor concentration, blurred vision, insomnia, nausea, fatigue and weight gain plus much more beside. The painful truth is that clinical studies have shown for many these pills don't even work, other than perhaps having a placebo effect. There are many studies showing how meditation boosts these important brain chemicals without the need for pills.

Endorphins. Along with dopamine have the greatest effect on your sense of happiness. Endorphins are our body's natural painkillers; they are released through exercise and the more exercise you do, the more are released. This is why sport can become rather addictive. But interestingly the level of endorphin release caused through meditation is even higher than through running for example.

Cortisol. Cortisol is the stress hormone. Luckily meditation reduces cortisol production. Cortisol is bad news as it can have a very negative effect on health.

What does all of this prove? Meditation and every single though you have, has a direct effect on your body, from your immune system to your organs, tissues and cells.

Sleep and Relaxation

Sleep isn't just about how many hours you get each night; it's about the quality of the sleep. Just as the old saying says its "quality over quantity." Your brain requires enough of each of the different stages of sleep to regenerate. It's essential to your physical, mental and emotional wellbeing. Scientists have been conducting studies into sleep for many decades and understand the mechanics well.

Melatonin production is increased through meditation. Melatonin is critical when it comes to falling asleep. Melatonin production is reduced by stress.

Rutgers University conducted a study that showed meditation boosts melatonin levels from 90 to 300%. Boosting melatonin levels with meditation is far more effective than through supplementation. This is because melatonin is required in the brain and melatonin present in the body cannot cross the blood brain barrier. This makes supplements completely ineffective at increasing the melatonin levels in the brain. In order to do this, it is necessary to give the brain what it needs to produce melatonin for itself.

When you can't sleep, beta brainwaves, that are also known to be dominant when you are feeling anxious or depressed, are at work. The more you become stressed about not being able to sleep, the more difficult sleep becomes. Meditators have far fewer beta brainwaves and far higher alpha, theta and delta brainwaves. These types of brainwaves create feelings of calm and heighten our sense of pleasure. They also allow us to sleep better.

Body

Meditation increases our energy levels, helps us maintain a healthy heart, improves circulation, slows breathing, decreases oxygen consumption, reduces pain and muscle tension and can even help with senior health.

Increased Energy. There are lots of ways in which meditation can help us to increase our energy levels:

Reducing cortisol production increased energy levels by around 50%.

Boosting the number of endorphins that are released increases energy.

Good quality deep sleep, the more energy we get, the more energy we have.

DHEA on of the chemicals in our brain that is produced by meditating is also known for its energy boosting effects. That's why it's often included in energy boosting supplements, which are a lot less satisfactory due to the unknown long-term side effects.

Growth hormone production is also increased. This is necessary for fatigue reduction. Because our body produces less DHEA and growth hormone as we age, it also becomes lethargic and easily fatigued. Meditation can help reverse this.

Heart Health. Dr. Carl Stonier, a psychologist from the University of Hull, conducted a study on 40 heart patients over the period of a year. Half of the group practiced regular guided meditation, while the other half simply received counseling. Six of the patients in the meditation group were removed from the bypass surgery waiting list. None of the patients in the meditation group died, despite many of them having been on the heart transplant waiting list prior to the study. In contrast, six of the patients from the counseling only group died from cardiac related causes. Patients in the meditation group were able to either greatly reduce or completely stop their heart medication. Due to the success of the study. The remaining patients who had only received counseling were also given guided visualization meditation as a treatment.

This study is not alone in these types of findings.

It has been shown that meditation can improve the circulation and heart rate. This is simply down to meditations ability to relax the mind and produce a correct chemical balance that naturally relaxes and slows breathing and heart rate. This, in turn, allows the heart and lungs to work more efficiently and get more oxygen circulated throughout the body and effectively lowers oxygen consumption.

Meditation is for all ages and has been shown to be exceedingly beneficial for those of more advanced years. It helps memory, aids the digestive system, activates the happy chemicals in the brain and improves brain function, sharpening and focusing the mind and it gets rid of stress. All of this is greatly beneficial to overall health at all ages.

Reproductive System

Premenstrual Syndrome (PMS), isn't just about mood swings. It also includes other physical and psychological symptoms such as bloating, headaches, insomnia, anxiety and depression. Almost every woman has experienced PMS at some level during her lifetime. Doctors have tried prescribing various medications to counteract some of these symptoms, which are really just a hormonal imbalance. Meditation can help by reducing tension, anxiety and depression. It can help the sufferer reduce their irritability and become happier and more relaxed.

Libido and Sex Drive. These too can benefit from meditation. When we are feeling stressed, blood is hoarded by our major organs. This results in our energy and emotions being drained. Sex is the last thing on our minds. Practicing meditation reduces stress and energizes our body and mind, thus boosting our sex drive.

Infertility. There are sadly many physical causes for infertility in both men and women. But there are also emotional causes too. When stressed, our bodies shut down non-essential functions. This can lead to a difficulty to conceive, causing a compound impact, after trying and failing the couple can become desperate to conceive. This leads to further stress and anxiety which only exacerbates the problem. Acute stress not only causes infertility, but it can also cause miscarriages. As meditation naturally reduces stress, it can produce significant improvements in fertility and reduce miscarriage.

Pregnancy. The many benefits of meditation are wonderful not only for an expectant mother but also for her unborn child. It is recommended through all stages of pregnancy to form a strong bond between mother and child. It also works as a natural anti-depressant, stress buster and cortisol blocker. The Mom to be will be energized, happy and getting lots of deep, restful sleep.

Labor. It is thought that not only the increased dopamine and endorphin levels, which naturally help control pain, but also the improved thought processes meditation produces, help the expectant mother focus on her breathing and on her body and senses. Visualization techniques are also exceedingly beneficial.

Chapter 9: Breaking Free

This chapter might scare you a little bit. Your hands might begin to sweat and your mini person might come and try to take over. Don't worry, just take a deep breath and follow where I'm going with this.

When you feel anxiety your bubble is too tight, you need to expand it. How do we accomplish this? We'll there are three ways for this. The first way is meditation, which you've read about in chapter 3. The second way is opening up your body. And the third way is to consciously do things that make you feel embarrassed. So let's begin with the opening up process. I want to introduce some bioenergetic exercises to you. This is something that has helped me tremendously in numerous ways so I recommend them from the bottom of my heart. I'll not share every single exercise with you, but I'll share the two that I use regularly. If you want more exercises, you can just google bioenergetic exercises.

1. First one is called the bow. What you'll want to do is to stand up and put your arm above your heads so they form a V. Open your mouth as much as possible. (A lot of tension is in the mouth so doing this makes the whole face relax.) Slowly begin to move your upper body backward, like you're going to walk limbo under a stick without actually walking. Still keep your arms over your head and your mouth open. You should begin to feel your upper around your chest area begin to shake. If not just move a little bit more backwards with your upper body.

2. The second exercise is called Shake and Vibrate. Begin with lifting your heels off the floor and bouncing them back to the ground. Relax in your body as much as possible (you should still be standing, though, so don't fall down). Do this lift and drop with your heels a couple of times and slowly begin to move your head, shoulders

and arms around and try to relax your muscles while doing this. Don't worry about following a certain pattern. Just shake and vibrate your body as much as you can. The sillier you feel or think you look when doing this, the better.

The benefits of doing these two exercises are that your body will become more relaxed. The tension in your body will disappear and this will form a positive circle. You'll have less anxiety, you'll be more confident and you now have a way of expanding the bubble.

Okay, let's go over the scary part. "Consciously doing things that make me feel embarrassed? This is bullsh**t, what a stupid advice, thanks for wasting my time". WAIT! Don't you think that's your ego talking? Come on, you haven't got this far into the book to quit now? You have more courage than that. Let's continue. Often times when your bubble is pressing itself on you the most, it's a physical manifestation of fear. You have fear in your body that is holding you down. Now it might not be the kind of fear you feel if you're afraid of heights, for example, this one is often more subtle. This one is more in the background, but you feel it. Your enemy within is taking advantage of this feeling. He wants to control you and knows that you are an easy target when you have this feeling. If you let him take over, then you'll become less aware of your surroundings and more self-conscious. There is a way to break out of this.

Have you ever done something that was "not you"? I bet you have, maybe you were at a certain dinner party, in another country, in a new situation and you acted in ways that you feel was kind of strange or maybe even a little bit awkward now when you look back at it. Guess what, you were not strange back then. You were in simply a different state. When you think of it, chances are you did not feel awkward or strange at the moment when you acted the way you did. You're bubble was bigger, maybe even completely gone at that point. You were not only living, but you were also alive. This is the state you'd want to be in. When you are in this state, you are a warrior of peace.

Remember this: No one can make you feel embarrassed or anxious, only you can. You decide whether or not something that someone says is going to affect you or not. At the beginning of this exercise, then yes you're going to feel weird and embarrassed and there might be little you can do about it. But remember the importance of awareness, just bring total acceptance into the moment. Accept the feeling in your body, your thoughts, everything, as if these things were not you. You are simply the one observing everything that is going on. Okay, so what are some exercises that you can do? Well I guess I don't need to tell you what makes you feel embarrassed. I think you can think of a lot of things. But here one exercise that you start with:

Simply go out in the woods and begin to sing loudly.

If you want to take this exercise to a new level, then I suggest you travel to a nearby city where you don't know anyone. In the middle of the day, begin singing while you're walking the streets. Make sure other people can hear you singing.

If you can do it in your own city, then of course that would be even better but chances are that would be harder for you. Begin to feel how you feel afterward. Your heart will be pumping, you might even be shaking. But what if someone asks me what I'm doing, or tells me to stop? Don't worry, that will probably not happen, but if it does just kindly answer them that you felt like singing and that you're sorry they did not like it. Do things that make you feel uncomfortable and always bring full awareness and acceptance into whatever happens. Don't try to control anything else than your awareness. Chances are you will feel more alive than ever before after such an experience.

Don't tell anyone that you're going to do this, chances are they will try to talk you out of it, or they might laugh. Guess what, the biggest enemy after the enemy within is your friends and family. Not all of them of course, but chances are that you might have some people that are holding you back. They are unconsciously trying to prevent you from breaking free from your identification with whom you are currently. In the next chapter I want to bring up something very important, so make sure to keep reading.

Key Takeaways:

- The three main weapons that you have against the bubble are mindfulness, bioenergetic exercises, and the comfort challenges.
- Do the bioenergetic exercises on a regular basis. Especially when you feel that your bubble is pressing itself on you the

most. Your body will become more relaxed after doing those.

- Do the comfort exercise and come up with more yourself, do them and begin to break free from the bubble. Your body might be shaking afterward and you'll feel more relaxed. You will experience the true feeling of being alive.

Chapter 10: How To Listen To Your Body: Somatic Mindfulness And Kundalini Meditation

By now, you may think that listening to your body is an extremely difficult process or even that you have no need to practice everything that was mentioned before because you already know everything there is to know about your body's cues to you. That may be true, but there are always things gone unnoticed by man people when it comes to their bodies. For example, there is one of the most basic responses our body possesses that we do not know how it works exactly and all of us have experienced. The flight-or-fight response.

The flight-or-fight response or else the acute stress response is a psychological reaction that happens when we are in the presence of something that is terrifying to us either mentally or physically. When this response happens, hormones are released throughout our body to prepare us to deal with the threat or run towards a safe place. The name of this phenomenon derives from our ancestors during the ancient times who would either stay and face any threat that came their way or flee. No matter the choice we make, our body prepares us to face the incoming danger.

When we endure extreme levels of stress, our nervous system is put into action because there is a sudden release of hormones. The adrenal glands are stimulated by the sympathetic nervous system and the distribution of catecholamines is triggered, which include both noradrenaline and adrenaline. The results of this occurrence are increased heart rate, breathing rate, and blood pressure. When the danger has passed, it will take between twenty and sixty minutes for our bodies to return back to normal.

Another sign of flight-or-fight response it flushed or pale skin. As the stress starts to get a grip on you, the blood flow to the surface of the body is reduced to start flowing to the brain, legs, arms, and muscles. This will result in you getting pale or to your face being flushed as blood will rush to your brain and head. Your pupils will dilate since the body will also prepare you to be more observant and aware of your surroundings during the time you will have to face a threat. So, dilated pupils will offer you a better vision. Last but not least, you may also sense yourself trembling since your muscles will become more tense and ready to take action.

The above was only one example of how our body works even in dangerous situations that we may not even know what kind of response we are having or why we are acting a certain way. Being in tune with our bodies and knowing how to connect with them is a necessary skill to develop and the process of doing so will help you find out more things about yourself that haven't paid any attention to. So, it is not always true that we know everything there is to learn about our bodies. To this journey, an important method we could use is Somatic Mindfulness.

Somatic Mindfulness will help us build a connection between our mind and body, especially in the areas that there was no connection. It enables us to use the responses of our body as a source of information about our current state and our emotions. It comes as no surprise that

Somatic Mindfulness is used as a way to cure emotional traumas since it can be utilized as a way to enhance our ability to regulate the nervous system by helping us release the emotions we may have help inside us unconsciously and feel them in a physical level.

Somatic Meditation is met in Tibetan and East Asian Buddhism as well as in spiritual Taoism. As the name suggests, in Somatic Meditation the main tool used is the body and in a lesser amount, the mind. The concept behind Somatic Mindfulness is that your spirit, mind, body, and emotions are all connected together. When you practice Somatic Meditation, you will feel less stressed, less pain, less anger or frustration, and it will help you get over past traumatic events. Essentially you will be free of all the things that are preventing you from listening to your body and live a healthy life.

However, you should be aware that when you practice Somatic Meditation overwhelming and painful emotions of a past trauma will come back to you in order for you to deal with them. Don't be surprised or try to end the session because a past emotional heartbreak or shock will have to be dealt with eventually and through Somatic Meditation, you will be able to deal with this occurrence in a controlled way.

When you start your sessions of Somatic Mindfulness, try exercising for at least once a week for a two month period, even though it is recommended for you to practice more than once a week. But if you wish to practice other forms of meditation at the same time, you can opt for a once a week session of Somatic Meditation. After you have finished practicing each time, give yourself a minute or two before you start any type of interaction with other people. You need time to fully acknowledge and take in the experience you just finished doing because sensing your body this way for the first time will be a powerful experience. For example, you will need to ask yourself how you feel after the session is over, has anything changed in the way you hold yourself? Do you feel any different? When you answer these questions, you can open your eyes and focus on the room you are in for a few moments to focus on your new feelings and take in your surroundings, on how you see the world now. Is it different?

Before you start practicing, stand up and ponder on how you feel at the moment before you begin your exercises. Focus on how your breathing is and pinpoint the location of where you have focused your attention and energy. For example, how does your energy feel when you focus on it? Do you feel calm and serene or do you sense negative emotions and by extent energy that makes you unsettled and fidgety? What do you need to heal? If you don't feel anything there is no need to worry or give up thinking that you are fine. Those emotions may reveal themselves to you later and if they don't, then continue because Somatic Mindfulness will help you connect on a deeper level your mind with your body, spirit, and emotions.

The exercises start with grounding. Stand up and let your eyes not focus on anything. Watch the room without actually seeing it. Then, raise yourself slowly on your toes and drop down to your heels. Keep up this exercise in a slow rhythm while at the same time thinking that all your weight drops through your heels. Keep this exercise up for a minute or until you feel the jolts of your hips and lower back loosen considerably.

After you have finished with the first part of this practice, take a short break but do not break the position you are in now. Then, create a small bouncing in your legs by using your knees and letting them bend slightly. Turn into a straight position by pushing backwards again and softly shake your legs. Focus and imagine that his soft shaking rocks your whole body and moves through your hips, up to your shoulders and reaches your neck. Let this exercise relax your jaw, your tail bone, and lower back until the duration of one minute passes.

Once your jaw, tail bone, and lower back are relaxed, take a short break and bring yourself back to a standing position. Let your hands rest at the front of your thighs while you start focusing on your breath. Inhale slowly and as you do that bring your chin forward and softly move your hips backward. Then, move your upper body forward so that you have created an arch with your back. Stay in this position for a moment, for around eight breaths, and later, as you continue breathing slowly, let your head fall relaxed down. Then, move your tail bone under and forward, around your back until you bring yourself into the position you were when you started. During this exercise, your focus should be on your breaths and your spine, on how it moves.

When the above exercise is over, resume your standing position and slowly sway back and forth as a bamboo does when hit by a soft gust of wind. You will feel all the accumulated tension leave your body. If you happen to feel little tremors on your body, don't try to stop them. This is the way your body releases tension.

In the end, stay still for a moment and focus on the sensations you have inside and are finally able to notice now. Can you feel more relaxed and less tense? Do you feel any different your feet and legs? More charged with energy perhaps? More alive?

Let us take a look at another type of exercise. Start by standing and letting your eyes look but focus on nothing. Place one leg forward by putting down your heel first and later your whole foot on the ground. Then, shift your weight forward and on that front foot without letting your back foot leave the ground. As you step forward, reach out with the same arm as your forward foot, with fingers outstretched. When your foot is on the floor, close your hand as though you grabbed something and don't forget to breathe all the while. When you reached this position, one foot forward and a hand turned into a fist, pause for a while and then, bring yourself into a standing position by setting your foot next to the other, by releasing your grip and letting your hand loose on your side. Do this exercise for two minutes on one side and two minutes on the other side. During this practice, keep your focus on your hand, foot, and breaths.

When you have finished with all sides, don't move and stay in a standing position. You may start feeling the sway from the exercise starting on its own. Don't try to stop it, but go with the flow all the while checking on how you feel. Does your body feel any different?

One last type of exercise, we are going to mention here is the following. Start by bringing yourself in a standing position and focus on your breath. Then, take a deep inhale and as you let this breath go, make a shhh sound with your mouth. Imagine you are telling to someone to keep quiet. You can even make the sound if you want to. As you do it, focus on how it makes you feel, especially on the area that covers your chest and your stomach. This sound should last until your breath is finished and then take another deep inhale and repeat the process. Keep in mind that this should be done for approximately eight breaths. The shhh sound is extremely useful for the opening of the diaphragm which sometimes is tight on occasions such as being afraid.

Next, inhale again deeply, and now utter the sound mmm, as you let your breath out. Press your lips together and find the appropriate pressure that will create the most vibration for your whole head. Keep making the sound for as long as you can keep up and then repeat the inhale process for around eight breaths. You should shift your focus on the vibrations caused by the sound that can be felt in your head. The humming sound can stimulate the vagus nerve which is the main branch of the parasympathetic nervous system. This way we will be able to relax by resetting the over-aroused nervous system.

When you are finished with this exercise, stand still and straight for a minute and check the sensations of your body as well as your emotions that may be new and noticed now. Do you feel any shudders or swaying movement? Do you feel the need to stretch? Don't try to stop it or avoid it, do what your body wants and move along with it. Do you feel any different than before you started this exercise? Maybe you noticed a difference in your breathing or any change in your sense of space? Maybe now you are able to put words on those sensations you experienced.

As we were able to see, Somatic Meditation is centered on the body and seeks to develop the connection of your body and mind as well as your connection to them. So, pay attention to your physical responses during the session of you practicing Somatic Meditation and with practice, you will be able to see more results. Awakening your body will have a profound effect on how you view yourself and will make you appreciate your body more than you already do.

One last method we will analyze that will help you start listening to your body more effectively is Kundalini which is a Sanskrit term which means primal energy and is coming from ancient India to teach us about a form of energy that has been roped at the base of our spine from the moment we were born and is also the source of our life force. Kundalini may be freed from the base of our spine by spiritual practices. Kundalini meditation helps you channel your energy and release all the stress that exists in your body.

Kundalini meditation is a part of Kundalini yoga and its goal is to move energy throughout your body starting from your root chakra located at the spine. This energy that is placed there has to be set free and go through all the seven chakras that exist in our bodies and then leave through the crown chakra that is placed above our heads. When we release energy from our body through this process, we create a communication path for the mind and the body to tackle physical, spiritual, and mental problems.

To practice Kundalini Meditation, the first thing you need to do is finding a location that makes you feel at peace and where no one is going to interrupt you. Keep in mind that the best time to practice is in the morning as soon as you wake up because the chances of being bothered are less. Another appropriate time for you to practice is at night, right before you go to sleep so as to destress and recuperate after a tiring day. Bring a bottle of water with you and choose clean, comfortable, and fresh clothes that will not bother you during your practice. Before you start, set a timeframe of how long would you like to practice, it could vary from a few minutes to a few hours. However, for beginners, it would be recommended a length of eleven minutes.

Take a seat on the floor with your legs crossed or even sit on a chair but place your weight on your feet. If you want to be even more comfortable when you are on the floor, you can choose to sit on a pillow or a cotton blanket. In both positions, your back should be straight. Then, lower your eyes slowly until they are approximately 90% closed. Regulate your breaths and chant a mantra to focus. A good choice for beginners is the mantra "Sat Nam" which means "truth is my identity" and it helps you direct your energy. Say "Sat" as you inhale and "Nam" as you exhale and as you do this, focus on the words you say out loud or imagine them being written in your head. This mantra can be also used during stressful situations you have on any day. You will have your own mantra that signals your breaking away from an old state and reflect on the state you want to be at the exact moment you chant it.

Kundalini meditation will help you let the everyday stress you may get from a hectic work environment or from problems you may currently face, go and turn it into peace. It will also teach you the right way to breathe and open up the capacity of your lungs. Added to this, you will be able to concentrate in an easier way than you did before and any random thoughts you may have will be prevented so as to not disturb your balance. You will learn how to be aware of your body and connect it with your mind and your spirit.

It is believed that Kundalini meditation can also help people who suffer from various addictions, depression, phobias, fatigue, grief, anxiety, obsession, sleep disorders such as insomnia, learning disorders, compulsions, and stress. It is important for you to not give up on practicing even though it may seem hard at first. All you need is more time and practice to be able to reach a level where you will be satisfied. We live in a world where we come face to face with constant change, even we change many times during our life and we may not even notice it. Practicing meditation in all its types and forms will let you tackle those changes in the best way possible, not to mention you will be able to identify the changing needs of your body. Imagine what it would feel like to notice any subtle change your body goes through, to know the signals of almost every need of your body. It would save us a lot of time and pain from searching what is happening inside us.

However, to take care of your body, you need to know how to develop an emotional resilience and constantly work on it. An essential part of self-care is developing the necessary skills to be prepared and face any stressful situation whether it is something serious or something light.

Chapter 11: The Miracle Of Mindfulness

If you haven't asked the question, then maybe it is time to do so now. While I am training my consciousness to handle a single point in time and space - who is managing my planning for the future and all the other things I have to think about?

That's a great question and the answer is a simple one. Remember, earlier in the book we talked about placing your consciousness in this present time and space. Well, the miracle is that, when you allocate the consciousness to the present, the subconscious - the part of the person that is infinitely capable, takes over the task of everything else. When this happens, you become superhuman (for lack of a better word).

The subconscious, and by this we are talking about the part of your mind that is connected to the universe, is capable of profound achievements and surmounting gargantuan tasks. If you let it, it will solve every problem you need to and render your life chaos-free.

The miracle of mindfulness allows you to relinquish your petty worries and concerns and focus in the present. In life, that is all you have. The past is no longer here, and the future is still not here yet. What your physical body and consciousness can tackle effectively, is only the present.

Most of our sense of instability and inadequacy comes when we tax our consciousness. When our consciousness is forced to do more than what it was built to do, it does so to the point of great stress and breaks down. It's like a one-ton truck carrying ten tons and ascending a steep gradient - something has to give. At first, the truck starts to heat up. It becomes inefficient and faces tremendous stress before breaking. Most of us lead lives like that overstressed one-ton truck.

The miracle of mindfulness does not require us to shun work, but rather shows us how to go about doing it with the right tools. Letting our subconscious do the heavy lifting is greatly superior.

Chapter 12: The New You – Dressing For Success And More

Earlier we discussed how to become less stressed at a situation at work – by using thought challenging to break down the worst case scenarios and by coming up with contingencies. You've changed your perception of the situation by applying a little logic and in doing that, you've become much more calm and composed. We've also seen how we can change our response to new social situations, making ourselves incredibly calm and relaxed when talking to new people so that we come across as fearless.

This is where things start to change.

In the introduction, I mentioned very briefly the 'law of attraction'. We saw how simply changing the way you feel about yourself would also change the way that others react to you. Let's take a look at that in some more detail…

What is the Law of Attraction?

It might seem strange but most of us will buy more expensive gifts for our wealthier friends. This is proven by statistics and surveys and it's surprising seeing as you'd think we'd want to buy more expensive items for the people who couldn't afford them on their own.

But the reality is that wealthier people have more things and have a more expensive quality of item on display. To get them something they'll like and to get them something that will fit in, we need to spend more on them. That and they probably spend more on us than our poorer friends, so we feel obliged to reciprocate.

This is an incredibly simple example of the law of attraction working. When you have nicer things, you actually attract even more nice things to you.

The same happens with money – you have to spend to accumulate and simply having more money means you'll make more investment.

But it also works with what you believe about yourself and how you act. If you believe you're highly capable at your job, if you genuinely aren't stressed by things going wrong and if you act accordingly; then you'll quickly find yourself rising through the ranks and getting to the top. When you have belief in yourself, so do other people.

One reason for this is that confident people tend to look more confident thanks to the way they dress and act. If you are very confident you might walk with a straight back and chest puffed out and you'll probably buy nicer clothes and spend more time on your hair.

Simply doing this will make you look like someone who is more important and who is more successful. Now other people will assume you are more important and more successful and unconsciously your bosses will be more inclined to want to give you more responsibility.

They'll also feel more confident sending you out to meet clients, while your colleagues might start turning to you for advice – because you look like you know what you're doing. It doesn't take long until doing all these things will make you the ideal candidate for that raise or promotion and then you become more successful.

The same is true for a guy approaching a woman in a bar. If he doesn't believe in himself and hasn't trained himself to be calm and relaxed, then he's going to be sweaty, nervous and unattractive as a result. If he comes over and he believes in himself though and can control his stress response, he's going to seem fun, confident and therefore attractive.

On an unconscious level, he is sending a signal to the woman that he is a good genetic bet for her offspring – he must be or why would he be so confident around her? There's obviously something about him that makes him confident, whether that is wealth, strength, health or intelligence. This makes him more attractive and the woman's neurotransmitters do the rest. Hello oxytocin, hello testosterone!

Change from the Outside In

We've focused a lot so far on how to change your mindset from the inside out but you can also change it from the outside in. How? By simply treating yourself a little better – dressing better, looking after your health and investing some cash in your own happiness and your own development – you can help yourself to feel more confident and look more confident to others.

There's an old saying that you should 'dress for the job you want'. Likewise, it they say that the amount you spend on your haircut directly correlates with the money an employer is likely to entrust you with.

So spend that bit of time in the morning to make sure you're looking your best. Exercise. And take care of your health. Women – try wearing a bold shade of lipstick to show that you're not shy and not content to shrink into the corner. Guys – don't go into work without bothering to iron your shirt, it just sends a signal that you don't respect yourself enough to bother – or that you're so disorganized that you couldn't find the time or the energy to do it.

Changing from the outside in is never enough on its own. But when you change both inside out and outside in, then you'll find the change is even more astonishing.

Chapter 13: Practicing meditation

When starting out, it's important to remember you don't have to be perfect at first. The practice may feel a little clunky while you're mind adjusts to the process and it becomes second nature. Put a little trust that it will get better once you get the hang of it.

In this chapter, you will learn the actual practice that you'll use for mindfulness on and off the cushion. We'll take what we learned in the last chapter and discuss what a normal sitting practice should look like. But before we do that, I'd like to talk a little bit about the practice I used to get me started.

When I first started practicing meditation it was with monks in a meditation hall. I was lucky enough to find some very hardcore practitioners only a few miles from my house, straight from Burma.

The first time I sat on a cushion with them was pure torture. I don't tell you this to scare or intimidate. I just want you to know that everyone usually goes through very similar stuff and sometimes, especially if you're just beginning to sit and using a cushion, it can be tough.

The first 15-20 minutes would be great. Then the muscles in my back would start to tense up, I couldn't sit still or find a position that helped and would spend the entire hour worrying about this instead of meditating.

If you want to use a cushion, and I recommend getting to the point where you do use a cushion, it's important to remember that your butt should be above your knees. When I use a cushion, I simply cross my legs ankle over ankle. Sitting cross-legged always use to bother me, even growing up so it's quite possible you won't have any issues. You do not have to sit cross-legged; you can use a chair or even lay down once you develop enough concentration to be able to stay awake while meditating. So a cushion is not by any means mandatory.

The reason I recommend developing a practice on the cushion is because in my experience it is the position that supports alertness and moving my practice to the cushion supercharged my practice. If you can develop enough concentration to feel relaxed and alert while on a cushion, you're on the right track.

One note, as powerful as the noting system we discussed in the previous chapter is, you cannot fight your biology. When I would sit on the cushion and feel the pain I would begin noting it. Sometimes, I would have a breakthrough and get past the pain and back to the business of meditating. But boy, getting through that barrier was very hard and lots of times it didn't happen. It can be good practice in discipline to learn how to deal with uncomfortable sensations and be with them with equanimity (something will discuss in detail in this chapter). But the goal of the practice is NOT to torture yourself or expose yourself to unnecessary pain. A little pain is Ok. It's also Ok to adjust your position from time to time if the pain becomes overwhelming.

When I was starting out, I had this idea that by becoming a master of meditation, I would also become a master of pain and ultimately have total control over my body. This is a romanticized picture of meditation. Sure, you will, over time, develop more and more control over how much you identify with the pain and other unpleasant body sensations and even emotions. We'll discuss how to gradually get better at that. But meditation and mindfulness are unfortunately not a panacea and you will not gain superpowers. If you're in a lot of pain, either adjust positions or stop.

This is not an excuse to quit a meditation session every time you feel uncomfortable. Only you can be the judge how much pain is too much and how much you're willing to deal with. In the beginning, I was not only unable to deal with the pain, I was also not willing.

I remember thinking to myself that I was never going to do this and that I would look foolish in front of the other meditators. If you're meditating by yourself, this will not be a problem. The real problem with meditating by yourself is giving up too easily.

So how did I get over this hump? The secret was simple. I didn't sit the entire hour in the beginning. I was taught a technique called Walking Meditation. When I meditated with the monks, we would chant in Pali for 15 minutes then when everyone was settling in for Sitting Meditation, I would get up and go to the back of the meditation hall. There I would do Walking Meditation for probably 15-20 minutes then I ended my session with Sitting Meditation.

In fact, in many meditation retreats, this is the formula for all-day meditations. You do Walking Meditation for an hour, and then you do Sitting Mediation for an hour. Repeat for the next 10 to 12 hours. This allows you to meditate for much longer than if you tried to sit all day long. No matter how good at sitting you are, sitting for long periods of time will eventually cause pain and discomfort that you'll have a hard time dealing with in the beginning.

My suggestion is to start with the Walking Meditation I'm about to teach you. It's easy and a good way to start any sitting session. Walking Meditation is often referred to as fueling your sitting meditation. Especially if you're tired or feeling resistance to meditating, Walking Meditation can wake you up, put you in an alert state and get the blood moving to avoid mental stagnation. You can use it anytime you feel scattered and need to focus on something.

These are the very simple instructions. All you will need is a room you can walk back and forth across. Turn off the TV and the phone. If you can try this out now, even for just 5 minutes please do because I think you'll get hooked on the power of this simple exercise.

Just a note here. We'll be using noting, but in a slightly different way than you would during Sitting Meditation. In Sitting Meditation, which we'll describe in more detail later on, you use noting to label the senses and thought. Here, we'll primarily be using it to label our movements. When walking, it's these gross movements that take up most of our awareness, so we use that to build concentration.

Ok, here are the instructions for Walking Meditation:

Stand on one side of the room.

Close your eyelids about halfway so you can still see the path to the other side of the room, but trying to block out as much of your sight as possible. If you feel uncomfortable, you can always keep your eyes open, but in the beginning this will help to block out external distractions in the room.

To begin, we're going to become aware of the entire body, all at once. Or at least as much as possible. So the first instruction here is to become aware of your body from head to toe, and as you're doing this, you'll repeat over in your head 10x the word "Standing." Remember, this word is really to help you block out random thoughts. It doesn't have to be exactly 10 times, but you'll find after a little bit of time you'll develop some rhythm and be able to count while saying it mentally and also being aware of your body. Don't stress over this. Remember the intention of the exercise – focusing on what you're aware of and using a mental label to help prevent stray thoughts.

After you've completed your 10 or so reps of "standing, standing, standing…" you walk across the room. We want to note all the movements of the legs, so here is the system to do that. First, the rule here is to move your body as slowly as possible. Also, you want to direct your awareness on as many sensations of walking that you can "catch." As you lift your first leg up to take your step, note "lifting, lifting, lifting." At this point you should have a leg bent at the knee up in the air. Follow this with slowly kicking your leg out to place it down in front of you and note, "moving, moving, moving." As your foot begins its descent down, note "placing, placing, placing."

Congrats! You've just noted in micro detail the entire movement of one leg moving up in the air and landing back down. Now do that for the other leg and keep repeating until you get to the other side of the room. When you get to the other side of the room there will likely be a wall. Obviously, you'll want to stop a few steps before the wall. Although your eyes should be slightly closed, you should be able to see well enough to not walk into a wall (or any other furniture). Stop a few feet from the wall.

Repeat the noting of "standing, standing, standing" for 10x as you become aware of your body again.

Now we are going to turn and face the direction we just came from. To do this, very, very slowly turn your body around. Again, you should do this very slow and have all your awareness on your body movements/sensations. As you are turning, you note "turning, turning, turning." Make sure you are focused on the body sensations that make up the act of turning.

Once you're facing the wall you just came from, you will again note "standing, standing, standing" for 10x.

Now you lift your leg, "lifting, lifting, lifting" then move it outward, "moving, moving, moving" and finally "placing, placing, placing" as you rest it on the ground. Continue this with each leg as you make your way back across the room.

When you return to the other side and are a few feet from the wall, you'll stop and note "standing, standing, standing" 10 times. Then "turning, turning, turning." As you face the wall across the room, you'll note "standing, standing, standing." And so on.

If you've been reading along with me, I know written out it probably seems a bit tedious. If you can, I want you to just quickly review the instructions, set a timer on your phone for 5 minutes and give it a try. Start with Standing, then Walk, then Standing, then Turning, then Standing and then Walk back across the room to start it all over again.

I can't describe to you how powerful this is once you get the hang of it. In the beginning it will feel a little clunky until you get the noting down, but once you do it may become your favorite meditation technique.

I hope you've actually tried a few minutes of Walking Meditation and have experienced some of the benefits. Let's get into the nuts and bolts of doing Sitting Meditation.

The following doesn't have to be done sitting. I explained some of the reasons I prefer sitting for formal meditation, and also some of the pitfalls. But please, if for some reason you have an even harder time sitting than I did, here are some alternatives:

Sit in a chair.

Lounge either in a chair or couch.

Lay down.

Just be careful with the laying down option in the beginning. I'll give you some specific instructions on how I do meditation laying down. The biggest drawback to beginning meditators who try this laying down is they fall asleep. This will not help your practice and has the dangerous possibility of conditioning you to nod off when you try to do meditation. We get what we condition for. So at all costs, be wary of falling asleep in the beginning. It will be more difficult to break out of that pattern then it is to avoid it.

Regardless of which position you choose, let's get started. Our object of concentration will be the breath. This is certainly not the only object of concentration – some people use mantras, stare at an image, focus on body sensations, etc. I've found that teaching this to others and in my own practice, it's easiest to get some mastery using the breath, build some concentration muscle and then explore other modalities.

So you'll arrange yourself in whatever position you feel most comfortable with. We're going to use a new noting technique to specifically focus on the breath. It's very simple:

Place your awareness on the belly, where it rises and falls with breath. As the belly rises, I want you to note "rising." Stretch the mental saying of "rising" out to cover the entire motion of the rising belly. Since you're probably already in a relaxed state, the breath will probably be somewhat slow. So it's probably a longer than normal pronunciation of "rising." Note that you're not consciously controlling the breath, just let it do its thing naturally and watch it. Sometimes people want to speed it up or force the breathing, avoid that.

As the belly reaches full extension, it will naturally collapse back down. As this happens, I want you to note "falling." Again, say the word in your head for as long or short as you need to cover the action of the belly falling.

This is the basic technique. Just watching the breath rise and fall using a word to cover the rising and falling of the breath. Remember, the majority of your attention should be the actual motion of the breath. Seeing it as a wave of continual movement can help to ground your attention.

We will discuss distractions in just a minute, but there is one thing that will probably happen shortly after you start practicing. You will begin to feel more relaxed and as a result, your breath will slow down considerably. This is good, even desirable. There is a drawback though, there will be times when you note the breath falling and then you won't need another breath right away. Since you're not noting anything, you're allowing some space for random and stray thoughts to leak into your mind. What to do? When this happens, I usually shift my attention briefly to my body and those restful feelings. I note "rest, rest, rest" and usually after 3 or so notings of rest, the belly begins rising again and I go back to noting rising and falling. I discovered that this little trick of noting "rest" quickly amplifies the restful state putting me deeper into the meditation session.

Distractions. We talked a little bit about how to handle them in our meditation system in Chapter 1. First thing is to try not to think of them as distractions. The goal is to note the most dominant sensory input. So when you hear a car outside and that becomes the most dominant sensory experience it just becomes part of that sitting session. You note "hearing, hearing, hearing" and then gently go back to noting the rising and falling of the breath. If you have a body sensation internally, you note "feeling, feeling, feeling." If you start thinking about a bill you have to pay later in the day, you note "thinking, thinking, thinking." Remember, we're not focusing on the actual word we use to note, but the sensory experience that word is referring to.

Remember, the entire purpose of the mental noting is help you focus on what is in your awareness at that moment. I said above that all distractions become part of the practice. This is true, but the caveat is when you decide on 1 object of concentration before a session, in this case the breath, you want to gently return to the breath.

After some practice, you'll find your awareness locks onto the breath so strongly that although you may still hear outside noises or feelings in the body, the breath will remain the dominant sensory experience. In some respects, this is a milestone you've been practicing well and your concentration muscle is getting strong.

Keep in mind 5 minutes of solid concentration practice is better than 30 minutes of scattered attention. That's why it can be detrimental in the beginning to meditate laying down. It makes it a lot easier to drift off into stray thought, fall asleep, etc.

The above is the basis for the entire method of meditation. Note the rising and falling of the breath. When something else grabs your immediate attention, note it away with one of the following – Touching, Feeling, Hearing, Thinking, Seeing (if you happen to see images in your mind).

One of the common worries of a beginning meditator is that they're "not doing it right" or they're afraid they're using the wrong words to note different sensations. There are no wrong words. The reason we use certain words all the time is to condition the mind so it doesn't have to do any extra thinking when we're noting. Remember, the majority of your mental energy should be on your awareness, not on the word you use to note. If you accidentally use the wrong word in the beginning – like use Feeling to note how your butt is hurting on the cushion instead of Touching, don't worry about it. Just move on. If you catch yourself thinking that you used the wrong word, just note "thinking, thinking, thinking" and move back to the breath.

I think it was Daniel Ingram that said in his book, Hardcore Teachings Of The Buddha, "When in doubt, note it out." He writes about how he would tell his teacher about all these amazing things that he was experiencing when he was meditating and the teacher simply replied, "Did you note it?"

The idea that you should just be noting everything brings up another important point that will contribute to your success as a meditator. Meditation is NOT therapy. You should not be analyzing your thoughts or body sensations or the meanings behind any of your experiences. If you catch yourself doing this during a meditation session, note "thinking, thinking, thinking." For the time you are on the cushion, you do not want to analyze the meaning of your body sensations or thoughts. This is not to say that therapy isn't good or useful, it just does little good during a formal meditation practice.

When meditating, we simply focus on the content of our experience, we are not worried about the meaning of this content. This will get easier and easier the more you do it and especially once you get proficient with concentrating on the breath. These types of thoughts will begin to decrease as you teach your mind that you are no longer giving those thoughts attention while you're meditating.

This is not to say that you can't spend a few minutes after your session to think over what just happened. Just be careful. I've been in group sits where afterwards people reported seeing intense visual images. Once you get good at clearing your mind, don't be surprised if some psychological stuff comes up or maybe rather you become more aware of the thoughts that run through your head on auto-pilot. Honestly, I wouldn't give a whole lot of attention to those thoughts or images. They can be very realistic and dreamlike and should be treated as distractions, rather than major symbolic messages full of meaning.

I will give you just a quick example of the kind of insight that may be useful after a session. One time I was meditating and had a flashback to the first time I had to do a book report as a little kid. I saw the scene unfold in my head and was right back there, sitting on the counter of my kitchen freaking out while my mom and dad tried to calm me down. I saw myself breaking out in a rash and they gave me some Benadryl. I hadn't thought about that in a long time. I finally caught myself, noted it and went back to watching my breathing.

When the sit was over, I wondered if that experience shaped later experiences of procrastination. Was that same pattern happening over and over? When I get overwhelmed or can't figure out how to do something my first reaction is to get sleepy and take a nap. Was that just me recreating the Benadryl given to me to take away the rash I got from freaking out?

While these are all interesting thoughts and analysis, I don't know that one thing is connected to another. It can be fun in this way to psychoanalyze. Other vivid memories have come up during meditation that I haven't thought about in many years. Treat these as an interesting side effect of meditation and try not to give them too much weight. Again, they're interesting and fun and you might gain some insight into things that happened that are still affecting you, however I would caution against giving them too much import. It could just be the mind trying anything to grab your attention and get back in the driver's seat.

Just one note on word choice above. When I use the word insight, I'm referring to the psychological meaning of the word. I just want to clarify that I'm not using it to refer to what is called Insight Meditation or Vipassana. Insight Meditation will be discussed at length in the next volume of this series.

One last consideration is the length of your beginning meditation sessions. You will have to play around with this somewhat. Remember how we talked about sitting and how it can become uncomfortable. This is kind of the same thing. You want to straddle that line between comfortable and uncomfortable. That's where you'll find your practice take off. This isn't to say you should spend 6 hours meditating on the first try. That would be extremely uncomfortable and probably lead you to abandon it completely.

I'm a big fan of using small increments to build a habit. But with meditation, there is a bit of a threshold you need to pass before you see real benefits. So to begin, I would spend at least 30 minutes a day to practice the technique. I would prefer to see you spend 30 minutes doing Walking Meditation and then 30 minutes of Sitting Meditation (all in one session to make up an hour). Try that for a week and see how you feel. Could you do more? Is it too much? If you need to scale back then do it, but keep in mind that a little bit of discomfort in meditation will ultimately lead to bigger gains plus you'll have the benefit of learning little by little how to deal with discomfort (a skill that is useful in real life). Do not torture yourself. One more thing, always have some kind of timer (silent of course) running, so your mind isn't worrying about when the session should be over. Set an alarm on your phone for 30 minutes and do the Walking Meditation. Then reset the alarm and do 30 minutes of Sitting Meditation.

The goal for your right now, is to do this every day for at least 3-4 weeks. I know an hour a day can be a big time commitment. But the good stuff is right around the corner. Once you get the basic system down, then we can move onto incorporating this meditation system into the rest of your life.

Chapter 14: Mindful Listening

This mindful exercise will help open your ears to the mystery of sound without being judgmental in any way. This mindful technique helps strengthen your mind and improves its defenses against influence of past preconception and experiences.

It is easy for your feelings to fall prey to influence from particular feeling you attach to what you hear. For instance, if you and your ex had a special song, whenever you hear the song, it is bound to remind you of the painful separation. Mindful listening helps you listen to such songs with a detached mind and no trace of emotions.

How to Listen Mindfully

You have to make sure you choose something you will enjoy listening. You can slot in your favorite music or turn the dial of your radio or TV set until you hear something beautiful and melodious.

1) Sit comfortably, close your eyes, and put on your headphones.

2) Avoid judging the music genre or thinking about the negative things, you have heard in the media about the musician whose song you are listening to.

3) Explore every aspect of the track. Follow the sound waves and dance with full awareness.

4) Pick out the dynamics of each of the instruments used in the song and appreciate each one. Go into the analysis of the sounds made by each of the music instruments separately.

5) Tune into the vocals and analyze the sound of the voice of the singer, the voice tones, and range. If you hear more than one voice in the song, separate each voice and analyze each one separately.

The general idea here is to listen with great concentration and intent so you can become completely engrossed in the music without any trace of judgment or preconception of the music genre, the instrumentation, lyrics, etc.

Chapter 15: Setting Goals

It takes a lot more than a talent or a gift to rise to the top. Achieving success is no guesswork. You have to set the goals that you want to go for and then apply the effort until your goals come true. But simply because you have taken the step of setting goals doesn't automatically mean that they will materialize. There is a science to goal-setting and there are many facets you ought to factor in. One of the benefits of regularly practicing mindfulness is that we develop our capacity of setting goals and increase our odds of reaching them. The following are some of the ways that mindfulness promotes goal setting.

Sense of direction

Most talented people are afflicted with the inability of determining where they want their talent to take them. This is made clear when they start consuming anything on their path and put their hands on so many things. In order to set a reachable goal, you have to have a clear direction that you want to take. If you are not in touch with your inner self, it can be quite difficult to determine the most appropriate direction for you which can spell danger to your ambition. Being able to determine your direction correlates with your ability to perceive your strengths. You want to align yourself with the direction that feels natural to you. For instance, if you're a pretty woman, you have the body for both modeling and acting. In as much as you can get into both careers, there's one career that you stand to gain the most out of and you're the only person who can determine which career is that. Mindfulness empowers you to have a keen knowledge of yourself and you would know which field holds the most promise.

Foreseeing obstacles

The cleverest person is the one who has an idea of the challenges that wait in their future. If you are an imaginative person, it is not hard to conjure up these kinds of challenges. But if you just bulldoze around and set goals without giving a thought to future challenges, you leave yourself open to attacks and increase your chances of self-sabotage. The great thing about visualizing the obstacles that lie waiting in your future is that you can learn to do it. No rocket science in that. There are various mindfulness techniques that will develop your mind's capacity to view both the good and the bad of the future so that nothing catches you by surprise.

Our capacity to deal with temptations

There are distractions and then there are temptations. The obvious truth is that not many of us are equipped to handle temptations. For instance, we could hold very high offices and then at one point corruption rears its not-so-ugly head and we are tempted to take part in corruption at the expense of our goals. It takes a lot of commitment to be able to turn the other way in the face of a temptation. As you come at your goals, your resolve will be put to test more times than you will care to remember. But it is not okay to always fall sort of integrity. Practicing mindfulness on the regular fortifies your mind so that you are able to withstand the biggest temptation ever. And this is a big deal. An inability to handle temptation could set off your ruin.

Focusing on the most important stuff

Setting goals allow you to close in on the stuff that really matters. This arrangement quickens the process of transforming your goals into reality. When you are bogged down by trivial activities, you lose the energy that would have otherwise gone into the critical areas. For instance, if you are a business owner, when setting long-term goals for your business, some of the most important things will be customer retention, profits, and product delivery, whereas the not-so-important affairs will be things like your staff and corporate social responsibility. When you separate the important things from the not-so-important, you are in a position to hasten results by applying more effort into the most important stuff.

Decision making

An inability to make great decisions is what makes the difference between success and failure. Most people approach decision making as merely a toss-up. The stakes could be high, but still, the person has a cavalier attitude and ultimately this proves to be a costly mistake. Great decisions allow us to utilize resources to the greatest extent possible and to make use of all opportunities. Practicing mindfulness improves our critical thinking capacity which is a huge resource during decision-making. Studies show that decisions made based on realistic projections have a far better chance of coming to fruition than decisions that were born from delusions and unhinged fantasies.

Empowered to face the future

If there's one thing that the mind tends to be deeply wary of, it is uncertainty. And the mind responds to uncertainty with worry and anxiety. But when you convince your brain that you will reach your goals, the anxiety and worry will fritter away. In that sense, setting goals gives you control of your future.

Makes you more driven

Imagine yourself living as a free man and without any goals. You just wake up and go through the daily motions. Now imagine yourself with a proper set of long-term and short-term goals, as well as visual boards in your office as a reminder of where you want to be. Obviously, you are likely to be more driven and a self-starter in the second environment as opposed to the first. Setting goals flicks on your inherent motivation. You won't laze around watching cartoons when there's more important stuff that needs to be attended to. It is through mindfulness that we increase our capacity to set goals that are going to excite us to take action instead of boring us into a perpetual state of indolence.

Progress monitoring

It is not enough to set goals and expect everything to fall into place. You have to keep monitoring the progress of your goals in order to get rid of things that are likely to discourage the actualization of your goals. Through mindfulness, we get to improve our capacity to monitor our goals and hasten it all.

Chapter 16: Ways To Find Instant Calm And Overcome Anxiety

While it's entirely expected to get apprehensive about a significant occasion or life change, anxiety disorder is common among nearly 40 million Americans, which is more than the incidental stress or dread. Anxiety disorder can extend from a GAD, which is serious stressing that you can't control, to panic disorder - abrupt scenes of dread, alongside heart palpitations, trembling, shaking, or perspiring.

For those with an anxiety disorder, it's imperative to investigate techniques that can help oversee or lessen anxiety in the long haul, similar to talk treatment or medicine. Yet, everybody can profit by different approaches to diminish pressure and anxiety with way of life changes, for example, setting aside effort for yourself, eating regimen, and eating a well-adjusted restricting liquor and caffeine.

Additionally, there are steps you can take the minute when uneasiness begins to grab hold. Attempt these 10 master upheld proposals to loosen up your mind and help you recapture control of your contemplations.

1. Remain in your time zone.

Anxiety is a future-situated perspective. So as opposed to stressing over what will occur, "reel yourself back to the present,". Ask yourself: What's presently going on? Am I safe? Do I need to do something right now? If not, make a "plan" to check in with yourself later in the day to come back to your anxieties so those far away circumstances don't lose you track, she says.

2. Relabel what's happening.

Panic attack can frequently make you have an inclination that you're passing on or having a coronary episode. Remind yourself: "I'm having a fit of anxiety, however it's innocuous, it's brief, and there's nothing I have to do," Mickey says.

Besides, remember it truly is something contrary to an indication of approaching passing - your body is initiating its battle or-flight reaction, the framework that is going to keep you alive, she says.

3. Fact-check your thoughts.

Individuals with anxiety frequently focus on most pessimistic scenario situations, Mickey says. To battle these stresses, consider how sensible they are. How about we accept that you're anxious about a significant presentation at work. As opposed to might suspect, "I'm going to bomb," for instance, say, "I'm anxious, yet I'm readied. A couple of things will go well, and some may not," she proposes. Getting into a case of reevaluating your feelings of trepidation causes train your brain to think of an objective method to manage your anxious contemplations.

4. Take in and out.

Deep breathing causes you quiet down. While you may have found out about explicit breathing activities, you don't have to stress over checking out a specific number of breaths, Mickey says. Rather simply center around equitably taking in and breathing out. This will help deferred down and re-center brain, she says.

5. Follow the 3-3-3 rule.

Look at you and name three things you see. By then, name three sounds you hear. Finally, move three bits of your body - your fingers, lower leg, and arm. The moment you feel your brain going 100 miles for consistently, this mental trick can help center your mind, returning you to the present moment, Mickey says.

6. Just do something.

Go for a stroll, Stand up, discard a bit of rubbish from your work area - any activity that intrudes on your line of reasoning encourages you recapture a feeling of control, Mickey recommends.

7. Stand upright.

"At the point when we are restless, we guarantee our chest region - where our heart and lungs are found - by slumping over," Mickey says. For a speedy physical solution for this typical reaction, pull your shoulders back, stand or sit with your feet isolated, and open your chest. This causes your body begin to detect that it's back in charge, she says.

8. Avoid sugar.

It may lure to follow something sweet when you're centered, yet that chocolate bar can achieve more harm damage than anything else, as research demonstrates that eating an excessive amount of sugar can exacerbate restless emotions. Instead of wandering into the treat bowl, drink a glass of water or eat protein, Mickey says, which will give a moderate imperativeness your body can use to recover.

9. Ask for a second opinion.

Text or call a companion or relative and go through your stresses with them, Mickey opines. "Saying them so anyone can help you to recognize the truth about them plainly." It can in like manner make your emotions out of fear on paper.

10. Watch an interesting movie.

This last technique may be the most straightforward one yet: Cue up catches of your preferred entertainer or clever TV appear. Snickering is a decent solution for an anxious mind, Mickey says. Research demonstrates that giggling has loads of advantages for our emotional wellness and prosperity; one investigation found that amusingness could help lower nervousness as much as (or significantly beyond what) exercise can.

Coping With Symptoms of Anxiety
Excessive Worrying

At the point when you end up stressing, ask yourself the accompanying inquiries:

Is Your Worry Reasonable?

Is the thing you dread extremely liable to occur? How might you be certain? Is there another conceivable clarification or result? Is it true that you are attempting to foresee things in the removed future that you can't in any way, form or shape anything about? If it does occur, what amount of will it truly matter? How might another person see this stress?

What is the Effect of Thinking the Manner You Always Do?

If your stress has some premise, yet there is nothing you can do about it at the present time, at that point check whether you can acknowledge the stress and let it go. This can appear to be hard for master worriers, yet attempt to state "There's nothing I can do to change this at this moment, pondering it will just make me increasingly furious. I'll acknowledge the stress and get occupied with something different for the time being".

Is There a Real Problem To Be Solved?

On the off chance that there is a reasonable issue, at that point you may need to concentrate on discovering answers for it. Great critical thinking can be thought of as supportive or versatile stress.

Attempt The Six-Step Structured Problem-Solving Technique

Write down precisely what you accept the primary issue to be.

Write down every single imaginable arrangement, even awful ones.

Think about every arrangement in down to earth terms.

Choose the most down to earth arrangement.

Plan how you will complete that arrangement.

Do it.

Did that help you take mindfulness of the issue? If not, have you taken in a superior method for characterizing it? Assuming this is the case, record the new issue and do the six stages once more. This is in the same class as drug for some individuals.

Chapter 17: Common Challenges You Will Encounter

Meditation is a practice which could easily be ranked among the "easier said than done" sort of activities. Frankly, when you read through meditation guides, it might seem like it is something that can be learned overnight. That is, however, not the case. There are many challenges that people go through, more so when meditating for the first time. Unfortunately, some give up. What these people fail to realize is that overcoming these challenges is part of the learning process. You cannot become a good meditator without knowing how to alleviate the problems you are likely to face. Therefore, if you can mitigate these challenges, then you will be better placed to focus more on the process of welcoming peace, love, and joy your way.
Wandering Mind

Of course, one of the major problems that most beginners face is that of their roaming minds. Yes, you might be ready and willing to practice meditation, but your mind keeps thinking of other things. This happens to most people, so you are not alone. This challenge could be in the form of unending self-talk. In this regard, your mind will seem to continuously talk about anything and everything that comes to your mind. Undeniably, this can be frustrating for a beginner looking to exploit the advantages of meditating.

So, what should you do about this? Quit? No! You cannot quit just because you cannot get your mind to focus. There are practical solutions to help you out of this situation. An effective way of quieting your mind is by counting your breath. When meditating, pay attention to your breathing. Monitor each breath that you take. Count each breath cycle you take to 10. A complete breath cycle will be one inhalation and exhalation. You can count the breaths independently. The idea is to have your mind focused on how you are breathing.

You may lose count in the process of doing this. What you should do then is to gently begin from the top again and continue counting to 10. This technique works best since you give your mind a simple task of focusing on one thing. That way, you will be less likely to swerve around other thoughts and sensations which are unimportant.

What happens when your mind gets used to the counting method and learns that it can drift simultaneously? If this happens, you should embrace the idea of reprogramming your mind. All you have to do is to alter the strategy. Count backward from 10 all the way to 1. You simply need to outsmart your mind. Remember, you are dealing with a mind that is rebellious to all your efforts to try and control it.

Lack of Time to Meditate

Maybe your reason for failing to meditate is because you don't have time. The busy schedule that you have to attend to could give you the impression that there is no time to meditate. Or, your meditation schedule could be interrupted each time you think of engaging in the exercise.

When facing the challenge of having to deal with a busy to-do list, you ought to mull over your health and wellness. Have a positive attitude toward your meditation. Why should you meditate in the first place? Ask yourself this question, and you will find the need to create time. Before investing your time in other activities, you ought to realize that your health comes first. For you to spend the rest of the day productively, your mind should be sound.

It is crucial that you meditate in a quiet environment. Therefore, you should make it known that such meditation bears a huge significance on your life. Inform the people around you that you should not be interrupted during this period. Making them aware of the importance of such meditation is the only way in which they will respect your privacy. If possible, meditate early in the morning when other people are asleep. This grants you ample time to enjoy the quietness and train your mind.

Spacing Out

Another problem which could be faced by new meditators is the notion of spacing out or nodding off. This is where one easily falls asleep during practice. This is a common thing that happens. It is easy for the mind to fall into a dull state due to its relaxed nature. Therefore, this is something that you should expect to experience during the first few days of your meditation. It should, however, be understood that this is not a conscious state of the mind. Relatively, it is a state when the mind is just dull. Nothing is happening here, so it means that you are not in a state of self-awareness.

A good reason why you might be spacing out is because of your lack of energy while meditating. As a result, to solve this issue, you should place more energy in the process. This can be achieved by assuming the right posture. Also, the exercise of counting your breaths comes in handy here. It will assist you to bring your mind back to where it should be. Likewise, for those who will use mantras, reciting these phrases loudly can help. If these methods don't work, then start your meditation exercise by experimenting with walking meditation. With time, you will grasp the art that you are required to master.

Disturbance from Visions

During meditation, your mind can easily drift because of the visions you are experiencing. Interestingly, some meditators might fail to see these visions, which creates a problem for them. One thing that you ought to realize is that the idea of seeing visions or colors doesn't imply that you are good at meditating.

There are great teachers out there who don't see visions.

To help you out of this challenge, it is essential to free your mind from any expectations. This means that you shouldn't expect anything to happen, including experiencing emotions and thoughts flowing in and out. People are different. Therefore, you should practice your meditation with a clear mind and be ready for anything. The only thing that you should focus on is the object that you should pay attention to. This is the training that your mind should go through.

Pains and Cramps While Meditating

Another common challenge you will experience as a beginner is pain or cramps. Certainly, you will feel pain if you don't sit in the right posture. For instance, if you are not flexible enough, crossing your legs together will make you uncomfortable. To deal with this challenge, therefore, it is crucial that you learn how to sit. It might sound silly, but rest assured it will have an impact on how you meditate.

Assuming the right posture of a prerequisite for successful meditation. The most important thing for you to mull over is whether you are comfortable or not. Maybe you are suffering from a condition that does not allow you to fold or cross your legs. Arthritis victims, for example, you have to consider your situation before settling for a particular meditation posture.

Keep in mind that there are different mindfulness techniques which you can adapt and still ensure your attention muscles are well drilled. You can meditate while walking or sitting down. You don't have to push yourself to stick to a method which doesn't suit you. Remember, technique is one of the pillars of meditation, which means that you should spend time experimenting on the best method that works for you.

Inability to Relax

Folks will be familiar with the scenario whereby they try their best to relax, but it seems impossible. The worst happens when stress mounts since you are unable to relax like you normally would. This is a problem which affects both beginners and those who have been meditating for years. We are human beings, and as a result, you cannot expect to be perfect each time you meditate. There are those days when it will be challenging for you to calm down your nerves. Nevertheless, with practice, you can learn how to do it.

Your inability to relax could be due to a number of reasons including stress, work-related frustrations, relationship issues, etc. When going through any of the situations, it can be somewhat challenging to get your mind to focus.

The first step you ought to take is to relieve your body from this state. Listen to your favorite music, exercise, go for a walk, or simply talk it over with someone you care about. These are ideal ways of freeing your body and mind from the burden of the emotions you had to deal with. Undeniably, you can't expect that meditation will always be a way out of your everyday stressors. You have to find external but practical ways of dealing with anxiety.

Feeling "Good Enough"

After some time, you will be happy with the progress you are making with your meditation practice. Once you begin realizing that you are actually benefiting from meditating, you ought to be very careful not to fall for the "good enough" perception. This is the mentality that since you are already feeling good, there is no need for you to continue meditating. Unfortunately, this can have a negative toll on your growth. The best way of handling this is by recognizing that meditation is all about developing a habit. The practice does not cure anything, but it strives to put your entire body in a relaxed state so as to reap the benefits that come with it.

So, never gain the mentality that you are good enough.

There is always a first time in doing anything. This means that it might take you some time before mastering how to meditate. Therefore, you shouldn't be worried that you are not doing it right. The fact that you cannot concentrate should not stress you out. Adopt the solutions which have been discussed herein to deal with your problems. More importantly, you should realize that going through these challenges is part of the learning curve. Hence, don't make any judgments and keep trying.

Conclusion

Experience is a memory of events that will never happen again. A passerby
Meditation has its pros and cons.
Having tried to independently go through the path of meditation, even if it is not long, we get our own experience. Pluses have already been described more than once, but the minuses. There are not so many minutes.
It is possible that the need for constant practice is the most basic.
Unfortunately, meditation is like a diet: you cannot stay for a while and stay forever at the level reached. He must either be supported or (and it is even better) to go forward. Both options require effort and continued practice. Not everyone has the strength to do it. On the other hand, we all have enough strength to go to the shower, is it not? Many of us still need strength to brush our teeth;

some consistently shave, then prepares breakfast, and eats it.

Meditation is part of the morning ritual — part of the hygiene procedures. Their "food particles" accumulate in mind. They must be removed. It is difficult to imagine how many minds carry loads from the past - memories, affections, offenses, prejudices, habits, opinions, beliefs. Not all of this is equally useful for us. However, the past has penetrated deep into our consciousness, cementing perceptions, making it difficult for us to be flexible enough to timely and adequately respond to the space around us, to the challenges that are constantly changing life sends us.

The mind is the most important part of the body, it provides our life, but how little time we spend on it.

Someone may object, but not everyone uses the mind completely. Some may say that some people have a less developed mind than others, and, moreover, remain in slavery to the body. Such statements are often found in yoga literature, for example. Those who have ever experienced dependence on substances or on other ways of avoiding reality may notice that the mind can fall into slavery, not only from the body.

This is a superficial look at the essence of things. The mind does not fall into slavery. But the mind needs stability. He needs a fulcrum. Remember the great thing: "Give me a foothold, and I will turn the Earth over"? This is about the mind. Any attachment, whether it is a dependency on social networks or food, work, or even drugs, or intrusive memories, anxiety, or remorse. These are something stable, something that the mind can be sure it can rely on.

Meditation allows you to change the balance of power.

Meditation gives the mind an environmentally friendly means of support that carries creation instead of any destruction. Are we looking for peace? No question, it exists. It is available right here and now. You just need to close your eyes, take a deep breath, then exhale by maximally mindful of what is happening.

Another disadvantage is the instability of the meditation process itself. This applies to the sitting practice mostly. Sometimes 20–30 minutes of sitting are easy and enjoyable. Everything turns out fine. The mind is in place. But sometimes everything is completely the opposite. The mind is constantly busy with something, no methods of returning the mind to the place help, and even the body. Your knees ache, or your head hurts, or your back has decided to remind you of your existence. And sometimes it's just too lazy to get out of bed earlier for the sake of sitting.

This minus is also a plus. On the one hand, it is possible that the body signals that something is wrong with the pose we have chosen and that we should change something in it or even the position itself. On the other hand, we are not locked into the framework of the need to sit for at least 20 minutes. We can sit less; there are no criteria for minimum or maximum time. There is only one criterion, the level of our care. We can sit for 5 minutes in the morning, a few minutes - at work before the start of the working day, for a while - in the evening. The main thing is to do something. In this practice, the action is important, not a reflection on it. As for the impulses to be lazy and stay in bed, the practice allows you to continue the development of self-discipline and the ability to achieve goals.

The mind often says: meditation is a good thing, but there is no time, you have to earn money. However, on the one hand, it can be perfectly combined. And on the other hand, when we think from the point of view of a long-term perspective, rather than short-term needs, we see that going beyond ordinary thinking is too valuable to refuse from it and stay where we are now, where there is no change.

What is the result of all our efforts?

Having achieved a certain level of control over attention with the help of the "One Breath" and "Series of Breaths" techniques, we continue to develop our mind control skills with the help of other techniques. We gain a whole new level of concentration. We begin to see more, further, deeper. We can understand the essence of things happening to us. We come to so desired peace. We gain a strong, solid foundation.

When we get into a difficult situation (difficult emotionally or mentally), we gain the opportunity to take a pause, not to get involved in the situation immediately. This is a direct result of the practice of meditation. Stay out of the way and wait. Do not respond immediately, so you do not have to worry about the wrong decision. In any difficult situation, whether it is a conflict in the family or difficulty at work, danger on the road, or an important speech. Thanks to the training of mindfulness to breathing and the skill of observing mental processes from the side, it becomes real to stop, to assess the situation, to see the future. Inhale, then exhale. As it grows in practice, it happens more and more often, which is very natural and organic.

Just as in the course of meditation, when the thought comes to stand up and go and have breakfast instead of continuing the practice, we have a choice that arises as a result of awareness. We are aware of the distraction factor and decide to follow the original plan. We choose to go where we originally wanted. The choice arises from the fact that we disengage with spontaneously arising fluctuations of mood, desires, whims. We gain real control, which can still be called the core. A firm commitment to moving toward a goal is what usually distinguishes a rich man with a spirit. Moreover, the goal may be the process of moving. In other words, the state here and now.

We worry less about the future, less regret about the past. And all because we begin to live more fully in the present. It is here that it is a simple but powerful tool, giving the opportunity to be happy. The point is not that we cease to face problems, the fact is that meditation makes it possible to solve them, that is, to act, and not to reflect on the causes and consequences. As a result, fewer unfinished, deferred cases, less guilt, and self-pity, less fear, and uncertainty.

"But it's not a fact that it is connected with "One breath" "and sitting in the morning," the inquisitive mind will notice again by no means. The discipline of the mind brought up by the practice of meditation can give even more than described above. It can be said that the above is given a more pessimistic forecast of the result than it actually is. It is absolutely noted that the skill to bring things to an end allows its owner to move mountains. And the size of the folding mountains is limited only by the imagination of the folding.

Another incredible result of the practice is getting to know yourself. Carefully and honestly watching their behavior, we can note the behavior algorithms that are repeated from situation to situation without changes. Some of them are not useful enough for us or our environment. Not immediately, but once the opportunity arises to try to do otherwise, change the algorithm, making it more environmentally friendly. In relationships in the family, at work, in work projects, in public life - everywhere we begin to see opportunities for improvement. After some time (for each of us this happens differently), the opportunity and vision arise how to act differently. How to refuse insults, from the desire to revenge, from gossip, from distraction in a social network, from usual other actions destroying our time. We inhale, then exhale. One breath gives us the right to choose. It is the one that we really need and not the one that is dictated by the moment of weakness, advertising, politics, other influences.

Of course, we still have questions about the practice. If there are questions, well: you can learn something. However, no matter how many teachers we visit, everything depends on whether we practice at home and on our own, on a regular basis or not. Everything else is beautiful words. The teachers sit in their cloisters - but it will not be any easier for us from the practice of others. Therefore, the most important answers, the most valuable advice are found there, in the silence of the morning seat, when somewhere outside the dawn, city or ocean, the stars in the gold of the dawn are melting.

Meditation leads to different results. But none of them is negative.

www.ingramcontent.com/pod-product-compliance
Lightning Source LLC
Chambersburg PA
CBHW072010070526
44583CB00015B/1424